Celebrate Winter
An Olympian's Stories of a Life in Nordic Skiing

by John Morton

Published in the United States of America

Most of the work contained herein was originally published in the
following publications; reprinted with permission:
  Vermont Public Radio's Commentary series
  Vermont Sports Today
  VFW Magazine
  Valley News
  Middlebury College Magazine
  Faster Skier
  Cross-Country Skier Magazine
  Master Skier

Printed in the United States of America
ISBN: 978-0-578-83912-7

Work set in Book Antiqua.
Book and cover design by Emily Newton.

Cover photo: Sean Doherty
Photo credit: U.S. Biathlon/NordicFocus

For my wife Kay,
who made the switch from Alpine skiing
and gave me a second chance to share my love for the sport.

Reviews for *Celebrate Winter*

John Morton's book *Celebrate Winter* is a must read for anyone who cross-country–ski raced in the 1970s and '80s. John is a fantastic storyteller and captures this time period with great humor and humility. There is no doubt from his writings that we were all truly amateurs and only did this for one reason: we loved the sport. For those who were not even born yet during this period, read this book to understand and learn more about the pioneers who paved the way for all you have today in ski racing. Thank you, John, for all you have done to promote this lifelong incredible sport of cross-country skiing.

—Trina Hosmer
First U.S. Women's Olympic Nordic Ski Team, 1972
Still racing at 75, with 60 age-group medals in World Master's Championships

---

Few people, if any, have the breadth of knowledge of the biathlon snow sport as John Morton, starting with training for and making the U.S. Biathlon Teams to the Olympics in Sapporo and Innsbruck. After that, he spent numerous times as the team leader or manager or politician for so many more World Championships and Olympics that it would be a waste of good space to list them here.

Instead, it's more important to understand the benefits of all of John's experiences as he recounts them. The biathlon sport—which is part cross-country—is a marvelous lifestyle builder due to good training practices, an excellent way to develop self-discipline, an easy way to find out and learn the meaning of competition and an entry into globalization when traveling to many various countries and meeting other competitors, especially those from different cultures. Morton recounts all this in his work here, and so the reader leaves with the impression that these athletes are not just people who ski around and shoot guns, but people who have the benefit of a chance for a wonderful, greatly varied life.

—John Caldwell
1952 Winter Olympian, five-time Olympic ski team coach, teacher, coach, author and founder of the New England Nordic Ski Association

With wit and wisdom, Morty's reflections on where sport fits in education, life and society will make you laugh out loud or mop a wet eye. Either way you will feel uplifted by the brightness of a man who inspired a generation of Olympic and college skiers.

—Max Cobb,
President & CEO of the U.S. Biathlon Association, member of the Executive Board of the International Biathlon Union, Chief of Competition for the biathlon events at the 2002 Salt Lake Winter Olympics

---

John's experience and passion for Nordic skiing and biathlon are second to none. As an Olympic competitor, coach, Olympic team leader and world-renowned trail designer, John has seen Nordic sports from every angle—and has the stories to prove it.

—Tim Burke,
Four-time Winter Olympian, first American to lead the Biathlon World Cup points ranking, participant in 12 biathlon world championships, including one silver medal

---

A treasure trove of historical commentary with endearing glimpses into the backstage of skier life, John Morton's *Celebrate Winter* brims with enduring passion for skiing and biathlon.

—Susan Dunklee
Two-time Winter Olympian, world championship silver medalist

John Morton has put together a remarkable book, based upon his broadcasts on VPR and his past books and essays. It not only serves the sport well, but it also takes the reader on a vibrant and rich cultural journey full of big personalities, sauna stories and large and small trials and tribulations. Trust me, these stories are true, as I lived many of them myself! A rare book for every Nordic skiing fan that will make you feel like the ultimate insider. It's a must have.

—Peter Graves
Eleven-time Olympic Games announcer

Wow, are you ready for the Nordic ski trip of a lifetime? Start reading *Celebrate Winter* by John Morton, a book written like no other in the history of the sport. Your experience starts in the back yard with skis on your feet and will move along as you read and experience what it takes to get to that ever-elusive step: THE PODIUM.

—Marty Hall
U.S. cross-country ski coach 1970–1978, Canadian cross-country ski coach 1981–1989, four-time Olympic cross-country ski coach and author

Table of Contents

"Skiing is not chust a schport. It is a vay of life"

~ Otto Schniebs, Dartmouth College Ski Coach, 1931–1936

(from *Reaching That Peak, 75 Years of the Dartmouth Outing Club,* by David O. Hooke)

Introduction

I grew up in the small town of Walpole, in southwestern New Hampshire. We lived on a hill, surrounded by pastures, with a panoramic view into Vermont. My younger sister and I would spend hours after school in winter, building snow forts, ice skating on the nearby Frog Pond and sledding down the pastures. Then, when I was ten or so, my mother got us skis, boots and poles from a local thrift store, and I was hooked.

At the time, the sports offered at our school were soccer, basketball and baseball. I participated in all three in junior high but wasn't any good. After school, however, I loved to pack out ski runs in the pastures and build jumps. I became very accomplished at side-stepping uphill.

A resident of our town was a graduate of Tilton School, a private boarding school a couple of hours from Walpole in New Hampshire's Lakes Region. Tilton was offering scholarships to potential applicants from northern New England. My mother had no interest in sending me away to school, but the Tilton alum had mentioned that Tilton had a ski team, which got my attention. I convinced her to let me apply, was accepted, and was awarded a 50% scholarship, which made it possible for me to attend.

In those days, high school skiing consisted of four events: downhill, slalom, jumping and cross-country. The Alpine disciplines (downhill and slalom) as well as jumping were the glamor events; cross-country was a lot of work. But for a winning team score, you needed strong performances in all four events, so unless you were a real Alpine hotshot or a special jumper, you trained for all four. My sophomore year, the Eastern Prep School Championships were held at Middlebury College in central Vermont. We slept on cots in the college gym, ate at the dining hall (in awe of Middlebury's co-eds) and raced at the Snow Bowl. By the end of that weekend, I knew where I wanted to go to college.

A couple of years later, I had graduated from Tilton and matriculated at Middlebury. I was both humbled and inspired to be training daily with some of the best collegiate skiers in the nation. I was also being challenged academically. One aspect of Middlebury I hadn't considered was compulsory ROTC (Army Reserve Officer Training Corps) for our first two years of college. I actually enjoyed the classes dealing with military history, strategy and tactics, but like most of my classmates, I found the Thursday afternoon drill sessions on the athletic field an embarrassing waste of time.

By the spring of 1966, the end of my sophomore year, a few things had become clear: first, the Vietnam war was intensifying and most of us were probably going, one way or another; second, my strongest results on the Middlebury Ski Team had been in cross-country; and third, (I had recently discovered) the Army supported a small unit in Alaska to train athletes to compete for the U.S. in the sport of biathlon (cross-country skiing and rifle marksmanship). After a few letters and phone calls, I was assured that I would be a promising candidate for the Army's Biathlon Training Center, and would be offered an Army full scholarship for my final two years of college, a regular Army commission, and a four-year active duty obligation (which would take me through the Sapporo Winter Olympics in 1972).

On the day I graduated from Middlebury, I loaded my car and drove to Indiantown Gap, Pennsylvania, to begin ROTC summer camp. That was followed by Infantry Officer's Basic at Fort Benning, Georgia, and finally, in November, assignment to the Biathlon Training Center in Alaska. I was able to make the traveling team that winter and competed in biathlon events in North America and Europe. In the spring, I took thirty days' leave to drive my car from New Hampshire to Alaska. On a whim, I asked a college classmate, Mary Lee (Mimi) Seemann, if she wanted to join me on the trip. Surprisingly, her parents approved, and by the time we reached Anchorage we were in love and decided to marry.

My second year in "The Unit" was much the same as the first, but I returned to Alaska in the spring of 1970 to find orders for Vietnam. In August, I boarded a charter flight in Anchorage and landed many hours later at Tan Son Nhut Air Base, in Saigon. After a two-week course on the current conditions "in country," a few phrases of the language, a refresher on weapons, and practice calling in air strikes or medivacs on the radio, I was shipped to the Mekong Delta to lead a five-man mobile advisory team deployed to "win the hearts and minds of the people." After six months in the field, I returned to the Army's advisor school as an instructor for the remainder of my tour. I was fortunate to get reassigned to the Biathlon Training Center in Anchorage, and in June 1971, I rejoined my wife there.

The tryouts for the 1972 Olympic biathlon team were held in Jackson, Wyoming, and although I'd had encouraging results in the winters of '68–'69 and '69–'70, I'd missed the entire previous year of training and competition while in Vietnam. Ultimately, I made the team, but was intensely disappointed not to be selected to compete in Sapporo. Returning to Alaska that spring, I served the remaining months of my military commitment, accepted an offer to teach and coach at an Anchorage high school, and enrolled in the local university to attain the required teaching certificate. At the urging of my wife, and with the support of Dick Mize (the administrator of Dimond High School, himself a 1960 biathlon Olympian) I decided to continue training for the '76 Winter Olympics in Innsbruck, Austria.

For the next three years, I taught seventh and eighth grade English, served as an assistant coach for cross-country runners and skiers, and continued to train and compete in biathlon. I had encouraging results at World Championships in Lake Placid, New York; Minsk, USSR; Antholz, Italy; and made the team for the Olympics in Innsbruck. Unfortunately, there was a virulent stomach flu ravaging the small town of Seefeld, which hosted the Nordic skiing events of the '76 Olympics, and the night before the biathlon 20-kilometer individual event, I was struck. I recovered enough to participate in the biathlon relay several days later, so my second Olympic experience wasn't a total bust.

Back in Alaska, I resumed teaching and coaching. Mimi and I decided to start a family, and in August, 1977, our daughter, Julie was born. A year later, a friend living on the East Coast let me know that Dartmouth College was looking for a ski coach. Although I loved teaching and coaching at Dimond High School, and both Mimi and I loved Alaska, we had family in the East and I was getting weary of teaching and correcting English papers every evening. I applied for the Dartmouth job and, as a Middlebury grad, was somewhat surprised to be selected. We moved to Thetford, Vermont, a short commute to Dartmouth, and began an eleven-year, challenging and stimulating tenure coaching some of the most dedicated and gifted athletes I've ever known. During those years I continued my connection with biathlon by serving in various volunteer roles, usually for specific events. It was gratifying to see several of my Dartmouth skiers make the shift to biathlon after graduation and go on to represent the U.S. internationally, including several Winter Olympics.

While Dartmouth is known and admired, across the country and beyond, for its rich, skiing tradition, in the late 1980s that perspective was not shared by the school's administration, and I felt increasingly out of step with the college. In the spring of 1989, I resigned my position, with no idea of what I might do next. Eventually, I stumbled into what has become a rewarding and satisfying thirty-year career designing recreational trails. To date, I have designed almost 250 trails of all sorts throughout the U.S. and beyond (including one in South Korea and two in China).

In 1998, I lost my first wife, Mimi, to cancer. In June 2001, I married Kay Howell, who had lost her husband in a paraglider accident. As an accomplished Alpine skier, Kay quickly picked up cross-country, and we enjoy skiing together every winter. Kay has a son and a daughter, and with my daughter, Julie, we now are constantly entertained and amazed by six grandchildren.

Most of the following stories were originally written either to be broadcast as part of Vermont Public Radio's Commentary Series or to be published as a monthly column in the regional newspaper, *Vermont Sports Today*. The thread woven through all the stories is skiing, which is also the thread woven through my life. I'm grateful for the opportunities the sport has provided me. I hope you enjoy them.

The Origins of Olympic Biathlon

My involvement with the Olympics for the past twenty years has been through the sport of biathlon. This demanding combination of cross-country skiing and rifle marksmanship is an event dominated by Europeans and Russians, while we Americans struggle. For many nations, biathlon is not simply an Olympic sport, it is a measure of national pride and a reminder of times when soldiers on skis literally saved their countries.

In any Olympic Games there will be biathletes from at least thirty nations, more than one hundred racers in each event. Three of those hundred will win medals, in competitions that are notoriously unpredictable. One missed shot, an error less than the diameter of a bullet on a target 50 meters away, can drop an athlete from medal contention to twentieth place. Sadly, there will be some phenomenal individual efforts that will go totally unnoticed by the press because the athlete didn't finish in the top three.

Another aspect of the Games that seldom gets enough attention is the friendship that develops between athletes, coaches and officials from rival nations. Ironically, while the media fans the flames of nationalism with daily updates of the medal count, the attitude within the Olympic Village and on the ski trails is one of international cooperation.

At the first biathlon team leaders' meeting of the Albertville Olympics in '92, there was a tense silence when the representatives from almost thirty nations realized that the warring Croatians and Yugoslavians had inadvertently been seated next to each other. The Yugoslavian team leader, noticing the anxiety in the room, embraced his neighbor, and announced for all to hear, "What goes on at home is politics. At the Olympics, we are all brothers in sport!"

A few days later, out on the course, a collision with a snow-grooming machine sent the Swedish biathlon team's waxing coach to the hospital. Within hours, the Swedes had several offers for waxing assistance from rival nations, and their injured coach received hundreds of gifts and cards from athletes of a dozen different countries. When it became clear that the fledgling Lithuanian biathlon team had no two-way radios, which are vital for giving the biathletes sight corrections during their competitions, we loaned them a spare set of ours. And during the final days of any Games, you won't be able to determine which nation an athlete actually represents, since most of the competitors enthusiastically trade their uniforms for clothing from other countries.

When he founded the modern Olympic Games, almost a century ago, Baron Pierre de Coubertin said:

The most important thing in the Olympic Games
is not to win but to take part,
just as the most important thing in life
is not the triumph but the struggle.

After six Winter Olympics, I know that de Coubertin was right.

Though a relatively obscure sport in the U.S., with only a thousand athletes nationwide, shooting and skiing is rooted in rugged survival skills. Biathlon, combining the physical endurance of cross-country skiing with the poise and precision of marksmanship, may well be the oldest sport on the Winter Olympics program. A short, carved, wooden ski found in Vis, Russia, has been dated at 6000 B.C. Images carved in stone of men on skis, armed with bow and arrow, have been discovered near Rodoy, Norway, and Boksta, Sweden. Similar sites in Russia and Mongolia all date back to at least 3000 B.C. More "recently," in 400 B.C., the Roman poet Virgil mentioned hunting on skis. These ancient hunting skills of moving quickly over the snow and shooting while on skis were incorporated into several northern armies and eventually inspired the sport of biathlon. The first recorded biathlon race occurred near the Norwegian/Swedish border in 1767. It was a competition between "ski-runner companies" comprised of border guards. A test of skiing and shooting prowess, it was also an important recruiting vehicle for skilled, local youth. Regular competitions occurred between 1792 and 1818. The first modern race was organized by the Norwegian military in 1912.

An Olympic Sport

On January 25, 1924, 258 athletes representing sixteen nations gathered in Chamonix, France, for the first International Winter Sports Week. Two years later, the International Olympic Committee retroactively recognized Chamonix as the first Winter Olympic Games. In addition to the five sports on the official program (bobsled, ice hockey, figure skating, speed skating and Nordic skiing — both cross-country and jumping), curling and the military patrol were presented as demonstration events. In the early years, only active-duty soldiers could participate in the patrol.

The military patrol pitted national teams comprised of four members — an officer, a noncommissioned officer, and two enlisted men — who skied together and shot on the firing range at the officer's command. The marksmanship in early biathlon competitions was complicated by shooting various distances on different shooting ranges, forcing athletes to estimate the distance to the target and adjust their sights accordingly. The final team ranking represented both their speed on skis and shooting accuracy. At those first Winter Games in France, it was military patrol member Camille Mandrillon who took the Olympic oath on behalf of all the competitors. The military patrol persisted as a demonstration sport in 1928, 1936 and 1948 until it was dropped, presumably due to public sentiment following World War II.

In the mid-1950s, Swedish officials connected with the sport of modern pentathlon, a Summer Olympics sport inspired by the five skills a Napoleonic messenger required (cross-country running, pistol marksmanship, fencing, swimming and horseback riding), began to promote winter biathlon. In 1958, the first Biathlon World

Championships, hosted in Saalfelden, Austria, attracted twenty-five athletes from seven nations. The U.S. participants had ties to the Tenth Mountain Division and Camp Hale, Colorado.

Army and National Guard Enter the Picture

When the 1960 Squaw Valley Winter Olympic Organizing Committee chose biathlon to replace bobsled (which could not be held due to the absence of a refrigerated bob run), the U.S. Army recognized an opportunity. Initially, in 1958, Camp Hale in Colorado was designated as a training site for the handful of U.S. biathletes, but soon a modern Biathlon Training Center was established at Fort Richardson, Alaska. Sven Johanson, a Swedish immigrant to the U.S. and Olympic Nordic skier who was said to have simultaneously held national championships in four different sports in his native country, was hired to coach the U.S. biathletes. Although the training center was operated by the army and most of the athletes were active-duty soldiers, the other services were also represented. While Alaska might have been a "hardship tour" for many Vietnam era draftees, it provided challenging training and endless outdoor adventures for the biathletes assigned to Fort Richardson. Until it closed in 1973, the training center in Alaska supplied the vast majority of U.S. biathletes who dominated the domestic competitions and participated annually in biathlon world championships, the World Cup circuit, the International Military (or CISM) Games and, each quadrennial, the Winter Olympics. It is not surprising that many competitors made Alaska their home after fulfilling their military obligation.

According to Ltc. Bill Spencer, a veteran of the Fort Richardson training center and a two-time Olympian who would later serve as the first National Guard Bureau biathlon coordinator, "The Army supported biathlon with administration, coaching, training facilities, and the opportunity for international competitive experience during the critical, early stage of its development here in the USA."

When the army closed the Biathlon Training Center due to budget cuts following the Vietnam War, the Vermont National Guard stepped in by establishing a world-class biathlon facility at the Ethan Allen Firing Range in Jericho, Vermont. In fact, the biathlon events at the 1980 Winter Olympics in Lake Placid, New York, were organized and staffed largely by volunteers from the Vermont and New York Army National Guard.

Soon thereafter, the National Guard Bureau and the U.S. Army established the popular World Class Athlete Program and retained 1980 Olympic Team Coach Art Stegen to train the growing number of talented National Guard biathletes. Art was a veteran of the Biathlon Training Center in Alaska and several international competitions and was the only non-Norwegian to be awarded coaching certificates in both biathlon and cross-country skiing from the prestigious Norwegian Sports Institute. By the 1998 Winter Olympics in Nagano, Japan, 75 percent of the U.S. biathletes were members of the National Guard. In recent years, the All Guard Biathlon Championship draws athletes from thirty states.

The Event: How It's Done

The biathlon event at the 1960 Squaw Valley Olympics was a 20-kilometer individual. Athletes started at minute intervals and stopped at four different ranges: the first three, shooting prone at 250, 200, and 150 meters, and finally shooting standing at 100 meters, firing five shots at each paper target. Large-caliber rifles, up to the 7.62 NATO round, were permitted. The prone bull's eye was the size of a tea cup saucer while the standing ring was roughly the size of a serving platter. A missed shot could add a minute or two to the skier's elapsed time.

By the '68 Olympics in Grenoble, a 4x7.5-kilometer, mass-start relay was added to the program, and all the shooting was on a single, 150-meter range. To add excitement for the spectators, the paper targets were replaced by glass, instantly revealing a hit or a miss. Every missed target resulted in skiing around a 150-meter penalty loop, producing dramatic changes in the running order.

In 1978, in an effort to make the sport more accessible to Europeans living in urban areas, and to reduce a significant expense of the sport, a switch was made from high-powered rifles to .22 caliber, with a corresponding reduction to 50-meter shooting ranges and metal, knock-down targets. In 1980, the 10-kilometer sprint event was added, and at the '92 Albertville Games, women competed for the first time in Olympic biathlon.

World Popularity

During recent decades, the popularity of biathlon has exploded, especially in Europe. In 1974, the first time a Biathlon World Championship was held in the Soviet Union, an estimated 120,000 enthusiastic spectators lined the course for the men's relay. In the past decade, biathlon has emerged as the most popular winter sport televised in Europe, attracting live audiences comparable to the Super Bowl here in the states, and commanding more, per minute of advertising time, than any other winter sport. And the International Biathlon Union has responded by adding more events, most featuring exciting mass-start or pursuit-start formats, which generate even more excitement for the spectators. At the Olympic Games in Torino in 2006 and Vancouver in 2010, biathlon was one of the first sports to sell all available tickets.

From Vietnam to Afghanistan

It stands to reason that with so many of our biathletes having military connections, and our nation involved in a number of international conflicts in recent years, that some Olympic biathletes would also have served in war zones. Bill Spencer, a retired infantry colonel, served two tours in Vietnam, both as a Military Assistance Command, Vietnam advisor. His first tour followed soon after his participation in the '68 Grenoble Olympics, but it was the second tour that remains vivid in his memory. Spencer had been selected to serve as team leader for the U.S. biathletes at the '72 Sapporo Games before receiving orders for his second

Vietnam tour. He deployed in July of '71, but was allowed to join the team in early winter. On the day of the Closing Ceremony in Japan, while the rest of the U.S. Olympic delegation headed home, Spencer returned to Vietnam. He arrived in the oppressive heat of Saigon, still in his Closing Ceremony uniform! His tour in Vietnam was extended to cover the time he had served the Olympic biathletes.

Former Army Captain Rob Rosser of Casper, Wyoming, was a member of the 1998 Nagano Olympics biathlon team. When asked if his Olympic experience had any influence on his 2003–2004 tour with the Fourth Infantry Division in Iraq, he answered, "Absolutely. As part of the division's planning team, I worked every day with highly motivated, goal-oriented individuals, whose commitment to the mission reminded me of my Olympic teammates."

Retired Major Curt Schreiner of Day, New York, represented the U.S. at three Winter Olympic Games. He was regarded as an unflappable competitor, especially dependable during the frantic excitement of relay events. He deployed to Forward Operating Base Danger in Tikrit, Iraq, in December 2004. He commanded members of a widely disbursed personnel services detachment responsible for everything from casualty reporting to oversight of awards. With a slight chuckle, Schreiner admitted that his years of training for the Olympics made conventional military physical training and marksmanship qualification easy. But the stress of competing internationally for many years prepared him for the demands of his assignment in Iraq.

Lt. Col. Duncan Douglas competed in biathlon at the '92 and '94 Winter Olympics. The focus and dedication that Duncan cultivated as a biathlete were transferable to medical school, where he earned his M.D. in anesthesiology. He is currently deployed on his second tour as a combat physician in Afghanistan.

Peter Dascoulias was a member of the '76 Winter Olympics team at Innsbruck. Peter retired from the army as a lieutenant colonel but not before serving a tour in South Korea as the deputy commander of the Port of Pusan from 1984 to 1986. "My Olympic experience helped me set a good example for my soldiers, especially in physical conditioning and long-term goal setting. We encountered frequent challenges and obstacles in Korea, but having trained for years for the Olympics helped me keep things in perspective," reflected Dascoulias.

Dan Westover is a noncommissioned officer in the Vermont National Guard. He competed on the '98 Nagano Olympics team and in 2005 was deployed to Farah Province in Afghanistan as an embedded tactical trainer with the Afghan army. Dan echoed the observation of other biathletes that being in peak physical condition was vital in combat. He also credits his Olympic training with teaching him to set long-term goals and thus avoid psychological burnout.

Lawton Redman represented the U.S. at the 2002 Winter Games in Salt Lake City. Three years later as an infantry sergeant, he served his first tour in Iraq. Lawton said the support he received through the Vermont National Guard to train for the Olympics gave him a sense of obligation to pay it back. Not long after completing his first tour, Lawton applied for flight school and in 2010–2011 served his second tour as a warrant officer medevac pilot. He felt the tough training that earned him a spot on the Salt Lake Olympics team gave him an extra edge in Iraq. He found the strong sense of teamwork in combat very similar to what he had experienced as one of the top biathletes in the U.S.

I remember attending a reception for biathlon athletes and officials at the '72 Sapporo Games, where I chatted with British biathlete and friend, Malcolm Hirst. He had just completed a dangerous, yearlong deployment in Northern Ireland, while I had returned from Vietnam seven months earlier. We both agreed how much better it was to compete as friends with rifles and skis for the glory of sport, than what we each had been doing for much of the previous year.

In fact, that may be one thing that sets biathlon apart from other Olympic sports: many of the biathletes competing at the Games have experienced firsthand both the best and the worst that mankind has created.

COMPETING

Showing Off

I've learned many valuable lessons through athletics. I know about dedication, determination, perseverance, and teamwork, all thanks to high school and college sports. But one of the most memorable lessons I taught myself, with a little help from a couple of friends.

During spring vacation of my junior year in high school, I was with two ski team buddies, celebrating the end of the competitive season by exploring central Vermont's best ski areas. That day we were roaring down the slopes of Okemo Mountain in Ludlow. In those days, Okemo was famous for the longest poma lift in the universe. When the ski patrol wasn't looking, the ride back up the mountain could be almost as much fun as skiing down.

The conditions were perfect. It was a clear, warm day in March, but the snow was still packed powder. Since it was mid-week, there were no lift lines, and most of the other skiers, like us, were students on spring break. My friend Jerry loved downhill and jumping. He lived to go fast, which was appropriate since he often had difficulty turning. Chris, on the other hand, spent hours studying the famous Stein Erickson, and he skillfully mimicked Stein's graceful, reverse-shoulder turns down every trail. I had neither Jerry's guts, nor Chris's classic style, but I could fight my way through a slalom course because I loved to turn.

It was not too far into the morning when we spotted a group of seven girls skiing together. They seemed to be following us, but I suppose, to be honest, it was probably the opposite. Once, when the lift line doubled back on itself, and we were close enough to overhear their conversation, we learned they were students at Colby Junior College. These were not just seven good-looking girls who skied pretty well, these were college women!

Our pursuit began in earnest. We followed them all over the mountain. We were too shy to talk, of course, or even make eye contact, but we were perfectly willing to impress them with our skiing on every run. I will never know whether they were just taking a breather or if they were offering us a challenge, but as we hopped off the lift at the top of Okemo's most challenging slope, the seven college girls were lined up at the side of the trail like a reviewing stand. My buddies and I piled into each other getting off the lift, totally distracted by the girls. Though no words had been spoken, their message seemed clear: *Okay, boys, let's see what you can do.*

Before I could suggest a plan of attack, Jerry threw his weight onto his poles, crouched into a classic Alpine tuck, and roared down the mountain and out of sight. We heard gasps from the reviewing stand. Even Chris and I were impressed, especially with our knowledge that Jerry couldn't turn.

Then, with a confident grin, Chris pushed off, carving a perfect reverse-shoulder turn right in front of the girls, smiling at each one individually as he swept past. He made the difficult slope look as smooth as silk, carving one beautiful turn after another all the way down. The girls were still entranced, long after he was a dot in the distance.

I knew it would be tough topping my buddies, but the window of opportunity was wide open. I would sweep over to the girls, as if exploding from a starting gate, throw in a speed check just above the first one, then fire through a hundred quick slalom turns in front of the group and on down the trail.

Everything went fine until I caught an edge just above the first girl. I toppled into her, knocking her into the second girl, who bumped her neighbor, and so on, until the eight of us were in a heap. Our skis and poles were so tangled, it took quite a while to get things sorted out. I was too humiliated to say anything except, "I'm sorry. I'm awfully sorry." A couple of the college women were not the least bit shy, however, and they let me know *exactly* what they thought.

I spent the afternoon trying to be invisible, avoiding any skier who looked remotely like a college student. Chris and Jerry had a great time skiing with the seven Colby Junior women. My buddies even claimed they tried to defend me when the conversation drifted back to the jerk who had knocked them all down.

I've pretty much resisted the urge to show off since then. Last winter, when I took my fifteen-year-old daughter skiing at Okemo (my first time back in thirty years), I half expected some good-looking, middle-aged women to turn to her teenager and say, "Hey, look Lucy, I think that's the idiot who nearly killed seven of us from Colby Junior College one spring vacation, years ago."

Celebrate Winter

Patty Sheehan the Ski Jumper

I noticed in the paper that Patty Sheehan had won another LPGA tournament, and that reminded me of ski jumping. Patty is well known as one of the top money winners on the women's pro golf tour. It doesn't surprise me that she's so successful at what she does. I remember when she was eleven years old, and her fearless determination was perfectly evident even then.

Bobo Sheehan was the legendary ski coach at Vermont's Middlebury College from just after World War II until 1967. Under his guidance, Middlebury's ski teams consistently finished well in the NCAA championships and provided plenty of skiers to the Winter Olympic teams.

Middlebury is blessed with its own ski area, located high on the spine of the Green Mountains between Ripton and Hancock. The focal point of the Snow Bowl used to be the intimidating, 50-meter ski jump carved into the mountainside, high above the base lodge. The hill record on Middlebury's jump was more than 200 feet, and even a terrified beginner could sail well beyond 100. The upper half of the in-run and the starting platform were supported by a wooden trestle. From the top, the base lodge at the end of the out-run appeared to be miles away. The takeoff was 10-feet high, constructed of logs, backfilled with earth. The landing hill seemed as wide as a football field, and was so steep that we clung to a rope as we side-stepped down to pack it after a snowfall.

In those days Middlebury was overrun with excellent Alpine racers, but a strong team performance on the collegiate circuit demanded top finishes in jumping and cross-country in addition to slalom and downhill. So, many of us with marginal Alpine skills volunteered to ski cross-country and jump. Cross-country racing was simply hard work, but jumping could be terrifying, especially on icy or windy days.

For several of us, ski jumping wasn't really a sport, it was a question of survival. We tried to keep our knees from visibly knocking as we sped down the in-run. We rarely actually *jumped*, but instead coasted over the takeoff, arms flapping like frantic seagulls. Any time we made it down the landing hill and through the transition without falling, it was an accomplishment worth celebrating.

Into this world of college men, bravely facing the dangers of speed, flight, and the harsh winter elements, entered the coach's eleven-year-old daughter. Spunky little Patty Sheehan trudged up the stairs of the Middlebury ski jump with her tiny Alpine skis over her shoulder. She had long since conquered every downhill trail on the mountain. As she reached the knoll where her dad stood coaching his college jumpers, she announced that she was going to give it a try.

"Why don't you ride the landing hill first," Bobo suggested.

"Naw, I wanna take it from the top," she answered brightly, and she filed in among the college skiers headed up the trestle.

At the top of a big ski jump, the tension can get thick. There isn't a lot of small talk. People are pretty focused. When they finally get in the starting chute, it's not uncommon for an athlete to double-check his bindings or his goggles three or four times out of pure nervousness.

Patty didn't know any of this. She chatted cheerfully with the tense college jumpers until she noticed the guy in the chute check his bindings for the sixth time.

"Geez, are you gonna check your bindings all afternoon, or are you gonna jump?" she asked with a mixture of impatience and youthful innocence. Embarrassed, the college jumper stepped aside and said to the eleven-year-old girl, "Well if you're in such a big rush, be my guest."

In response, Patty wrinkled her nose at him, grabbed the railing and launched herself down the in-run. She held her downhill tuck through the air, disappeared over the knoll, and seconds later emerged as a tiny dot rocketing toward the base lodge.

She loved it. From that day on, anytime the jump was packed out, you could be pretty sure Patty Sheehan would be riding it on her Alpine skis, laughing and joking with the college jumpers.

It was fifteen years later when I learned that Patty had become a professional golfer. Certainly, there are dozens of extremely talented and dedicated women on the LPGA tour. But it's no surprise to me that Patty Sheehan is one of the best. I saw her poise, self-confidence and athletic ability when she was an eleven-year-old ski jumper.

February Memories

When I think of February, most of my memories are of skiing. As a member of the U.S. biathlon team, I had the good fortune to participate in several Winter Olympic Games, in different capacities, but always in February. Although those Olympic experiences are unforgettable, I probably had more fun during the fifteen years I participated on the Eastern intercollegiate winter carnival circuit, first as a competitor for Middlebury, then as a coach at Dartmouth.

Fred Harris, who graduated from Dartmouth in 1911, is credited with founding the Dartmouth Outing Club and creating the winter carnival, featuring sporting events and social activities to break up the long, cold Hanover winter. The concept was a success from the beginning. In the years prior to World War II, a young woman's selection as Dartmouth's winter carnival queen was equivalent to winning a national beauty pageant, while skiing events routinely attracted the top competitors in the country.

The years following World War II, when many of the collegiate skiers and coaches were combat veterans, instilled a sense of joy and comradery on the winter carnival circuit that survived several decades.

In the winter of 1965, as a freshman on the Middlebury Ski Team, I experienced my first winter carnivals. In those days, there were few specialists. Most team members were expected to be proficient in all four events: downhill, slalom, jumping and cross-country. Typically a college team might have a couple of Alpine (downhill and slalom) hotshots, as well as one or two guys who just jumped, while everyone else would be prepared to fill in where needed. This meant lots of scrambling to change clothes and gear between events.

Once, at the Saint Lawrence Carnival, a group of us had completed an inspection of the cross-country course, and had worked our way to the top of the landing hill of the 50-meter jump, where our coach, Bobo Sheehan was swapping stories with Saint Lawrence's Bob Axtell. As we gingerly approached the massive, hard-packed knoll, jumpers rocketed from the takeoff, just over our heads, and sailed out of sight down the hill. We waited for instructions while the conversation between the coaches grew more animated. With a grin, Bobo called over to us, "Hey boys, Ax here doesn't think you can ride the landing hill on your x-c boards. I bet him he's wrong!"

Although heading down the rutted, bullet-proof landing hill on fragile, birch and hickory cross-country skis seemed like suicide, it was clear to the Middlebury skiers that our participation was not optional. Miraculously, we all survived, although I have never been more terrified on skis. Bobo was in great spirits that evening, probably because Axtell would be buying the beer for quite a while.

The Dartmouth Carnival was always the premier event, partly because of its tradition, and also because it garnered national attention. Dartmouth dominated the skiing scene in those years, but at the 1965 Winter Carnival, Middlebury eked out a victory, an especially painful loss for the Greenies.

Following two days of hotly contested skiing events, the Outing Club hosted a lavish awards banquet attended by several of the school's administrators. Following a delicious meal and the prerequisite speeches, the beautiful carnival queen was escorted to the impressive prize table, laden with gleaming silver medals, mugs and bowls. Smiling regally, she prepared to hand out the hardware to the top competitors in each of the events, as her carnival date beamed with pride from the head table.

Gordie Eaton, Middlebury's top Alpine skier, drew his teammates together and whispered, "If you go up for an award, you'd better kiss the queen, or you won't be riding home in our van!" The first timid pecks on her cheek by Middlebury skiers were greeted with cheers from the other skiers, and soon every award recipient was planting a big smooch on the royal lips. Her Majesty was a good sport and seemed to be enjoying herself, but when Gordie bolted to the front of the hall for his award, ignored the silver bowl, swept the queen off her feet, and headed for the door, her date had to be restrained.

Then there was the Williams College Carnival tradition of racing back from the cross-country event to the locker room for a steaming hot shower followed by a sprint down the hall to the swimming pool for a skinny dip. This tradition became the stuff of legend when the naked skiers dove into the middle of an intercollegiate swim meet, but that's another story...

The Frogman and the Physicist

The Scandinavian sauna bath is as much a part of Nordic skiing as snow. When I was at the U.S. Biathlon Training Center at Fort Richardson, Alaska, in the late 1960s and early '70s, the coach of the team was a Swedish immigrant to the U.S. named Sven Johanson, and he made the sauna part of our training schedule. As a result, we experienced some of the most impressive saunas in North America and Europe. But the most memorable was a sauna we constructed under Sven's careful supervision at Independence Mines in Alaska's Talkeetna Mountains.

Each autumn, Sven loaded a couple of Army trucks full of supplies and his twenty young biathletes, and drove north from Anchorage to find snow. At Palmer, made famous in 1994 as the home of Olympic downhill champion, Tommy Moe, we left the highway and followed a gravel road high into the Talkeetnas. An hour later, after countless switchbacks, we arrived at Independence Mines, a collection of rundown bunk houses and mining sheds, abandoned when the price of gold plummeted after World War II.

We were so high in the peaks that the lights of Palmer, far below in the Matanuska Valley, twinkled like stars. But even in this remote training site, Sven had to have a sauna. He damned a mountain stream, creating a deep pool. Then, enlisting the help of the entire team, he scavenged wood from fallen mine buildings and built a sauna over the pool. Since Sven was a plumber by trade, the hot room was heated with a huge plumber's torch, fueled by propane, and thrust through a hole near the bottom of a 55-gallon drum full of rocks.

One of our workouts was to jog 5 miles down the valley to the Little Susitna River, fill our backpacks with rocks, which Sven had carefully selected, and hike them back up the mountain.

Typically, as we went out for our afternoon training, someone went to fire up the sauna. By the time we returned at dark, the steel barrel was bright red and the rocks were dancing. Next to the hot room was a changing area, complete with benches and even pegs on the wall for our clothes. Near the door to the hot room, a hole had been cut through the floor providing direct access to the icy pool below. The athlete assigned to fire the torch was also expected to chop a hole through the ice with an ax.

We competed at everything, and the sauna was no exception. Normally we started together, the macho guys fighting for a seat on the hottest upper bench. Then everyone just hung on, trying desperately to avoid being the first to succumb to the heat and scramble for the door. The rest of us would act disinterested, but we listened intently to the gasping and wheezing coming from the ice water pool. The instant the splashing subsided, indicating our teammate had left the water, someone else made for the door and the welcome relief of the ice water.

Although most of us were in the Army, John Hall was our token sailor, an authentic Navy SEAL. He was not the most experienced skier on the team, but no one questioned his physical conditioning. I remember resting on a bench in the changing room, recovering from an icy plunge, when Frogman emerged from the hot room, looking like a boiled lobster. As he lowered himself through the hole in the floor, he put a finger to his lips, and gave me a grin. After the normal interval of gasping and splashing, the pool became silent, but Frogman hadn't resurfaced.

I watched the hole in the floor in disbelief as George Tuthill staggered from the hot room. George was a wiry athlete who had skied for Williams College while earning honors as a physics major. He was an analytical, no nonsense, kind of guy. He groped blindly for the hole in the floor and lowered himself below the surface. There was the normal splashing and gasping...then a deafening bellow! George rose straight out of the brash like a bright pink Poseidon missile. He landed on the floor stammering and sputtering. He pointed frantically to the hole in the floor, but his stuttering was unintelligible for several minutes.

Eventually Frogman surfaced, shivering, but grinning from ear to ear. George recovered his normal speech patterns, and for many years was a respected professor of physics at a University in Montana. He is one of the only Nordic skiers I know who doesn't enjoy a good sauna after a day of skiing.

The Legacy of Annie Oakley

I've been involved with the sport of winter biathlon for almost thirty years and, consequently, have spent a lot of time shooting rifles. As a member of the U.S. Team, back in the days of wooden skis and knicker socks, it was not unusual for us to fire 200 rounds of ammunition a day for weeks on end.

After retiring from competition in 1976, I coached at scores of training camps, clinics, and team selection races. I watched hundreds of athletes on shooting ranges across the country: from young novices to seasoned, Olympic veterans. And over the years I have arrived at a surprising conclusion: I believe that women are instinctively better shooters than men. The scientists would be quick to point out that my evidence is purely anecdotal, but I have no doubt that a randomly selected group of high school girls, with little or no marksmanship experience, would beat their male classmates in a shooting match every time.

I vividly remember a junior biathlon training camp, held at Squaw Valley, California, sometime in the 1970s. It was evident that women's biathlon would soon be included on the international schedule, so we invited several of the nation's most promising young cross-country skiers, both male and female, to a camp designed to promote marksmanship. These kids came from across the country, Alaska to Maine. The girls were at a disadvantage from the outset because the rifles were heavy, about 10 pounds, and the man-sized stocks were so long that most of the girls had difficulty establishing a comfortable shooting position. Nevertheless, these teenaged beginners outperformed their male counterparts on the shooting range throughout the training camp. The coaching staff worked overtime soothing bruised male egos.

But the incident that convinced me beyond a doubt that women are better natural shooters involved my wife, Mimi. When I was a competitor, athletes assigned to the U. S. Biathlon Training Center in Anchorage would migrate to Seward, Alaska, each June in preparation for the annual race up Mount Marathon. Seward is a picturesque village on the shore of

Resurrection Bay, surrounded by snowcapped peaks and hanging glaciers. The Fourth of July run up Mount Marathon, across impressive snowfields, and back down to the center of town, had become one of Alaska's premier sporting events, and the biathlon team trained for it seriously.

But we couldn't ignore our shooting for the month of June, so we brought our rifles and cobbled together a makeshift range at the Seward Town Dump. We stapled paper targets to discarded boards, moved back 150 meters to the firing line, and conducted our shooting workouts. As an exciting finale to these sessions, we set bottles and cans on the lumber frames, returned to the firing line, and shot from the standing position, until all the containers had been hit. A coke can, a football field and a half away, makes a pretty challenging target. There were outrageous bets, cheering and hooting as we aimed, shot and reloaded until the only remaining target was a tiny, bright blue, Noxema Skin Cream jar.

After several futile attempts, some of my teammates gave up in frustration. Others settled into solid standing positions, carefully estimated the wind, adjusted their sights, and patiently squeezed off their shots. The Noxema jar sat there, defiantly. A few more national team athletes shook their heads, and put their rifles away.

Then Mimi, who had been quietly observing the entire workout, innocently asked, "Can I try?"

There were indulgent smiles from my teammates as I reloaded and hefted the heavy rifle to her shoulder. She took a breath and held it. The barrel wobbled as she squinted through the sights. She squeezed the trigger. The rifle jumped against her shoulder. The tiny Noxema jar exploded.

"That was fun," she said, handing the rifle back with a broad grin. The entire U.S. biathlon team stared at her in disbelief. No one spoke a word as we packed our gear and left the dump. Another case of damaged male egos.

Mimi never shot much since that day in Seward, but I certainly couldn't blame her. Many times since then I've wished I'd had her self-control and known enough to quit when I was ahead.

Endurance Feeding

It's pretty widely accepted among endurance athletes that the well-conditioned human can function aerobically at a top level for about an hour before running low on stored glycogen, or blood sugar. In other words, a marathoner will "hit the wall" sometime after 60 minutes, unless the runner refuels during the competition.

In the old days, water, or tea, and orange slices were the most widely accepted form of fuel during an endurance event. Long-distance cyclists discovered that bananas were an excellent source of carbohydrates and potassium. They were easy to peel, and best of all, soft enough to chew and swallow quickly, even while peddling at race pace. Unfortunately, bananas aren't quite as convenient in the winter during ski races. I had heard about their nutritional value, so I eagerly grabbed a chunk of peeled banana from a feed table halfway through a 50-kilometer ski marathon. I popped it in my mouth expecting to mush it around a bit between breaths, then gump it down. Big surprise! Bananas freeze solid. Getting one down your throat in a ski race is like gnawing on a carrot. Through decades of racing, three memorable feeds stand out.

I have a ski racing buddy who is into natural foods. Prior to the 1990 Masters National Championship 50 kilometer in Sun Valley, Idaho, we were planning our refueling stops. We would race a 17-kilometer loop three times. Another friend had offered to haul our feeds to the far end of the course. My racing buddy had discovered an organic variety of Fig Newtons that he swore provided instant, healthy energy. I gently suggested they seemed a little dry, and that 42 kilometers into the race they might be difficult to swallow. He was insulted.

I filled three small plastic bottles, the first two with an electrolyte replacement drink and the third with de-fizzed Coca Cola. I figured that late in the race I would welcome the jolt of sugar and caffeine.

All went as planned. Our friend was at the far end of the trail, and each time I passed, he handed me a bottle. It was a lifesaver, especially the Coke on the final lap. I was wondering how my racing buddy was doing with his Fig Newtons when I skied through a pile of them scattered across the trail. At the finish line he admitted it was like gagging on a mouthful of sawdust. It's ironic that in a sport as healthy as cross-country skiing, sometimes it's Coca Cola that gets you to the finish line.

At the 1974 North American championships in Thunder Bay, Ontario, there had been marginal snowfall that winter in the Midwest and the 5-kilometer loop we were to ski six times for the men's 30 kilometer was bulletproof and treacherous. Early in the race I caught fleeting glimpses of other competitors off in the trees with broken equipment. As I came through the start/finish area to start my third loop, the coach jogged beside me and handed me a small plastic baby bottle filled with dark liquid.

"Morty, you're in fifth place! Most of the top guys have crashed. Drink this and stay on your feet."

I gagged down the thick liquid and kept skiing. Not long thereafter, I felt a jolt of energy and was able to pick up the pace. As I approached the start/finish area for the third time, I scanned the crowd for the coach and the powerful feed. By my fifth lap, I felt like a heroin addict desperate for another fix.

I was able to maintain my fifth place in that championship, which was a very strong result for me, especially under such challenging skiing conditions. After the race, the coach told me the feed consisted of de-fizzed Coca Cola mixed 50/50 with Coke syrup, pretty much the highest concentration of caffeine and sugar you can ingest in liquid form. Though it was not illegal at the time, the team doctor soon thereafter put an end to that concoction, fearing it could cause heart problems in athletes under such duress. It gave me a vivid appreciation of how effective doping could be in endurance sports.

Today we have a wide variety of scientifically engineered competition drinks that provide precisely the correct balance of electrolyte replacement, glucose, and fluid. But years ago, at of the Biathlon Training Center in Alaska, we concocted our own feeds. Mine was a thick combination of Tang, tea, and honey.

During a long, hot, road race in Fairbanks in the summer of 1971, I asked my wife, Mimi, to stand a couple of miles before the finish with my special mixture. I was running pretty well, in spite of the unseasonable Fairbanks heat, but my biathlon teammate, Terry Aldrich, who for three decades coached the Middlebury College Ski Team, was steadily gaining on me.

As I approached Mimi, who waited at the roadside with the critical feed, I struggled with an ethical decision. If I shared the mixture with Aldrich, he would almost certainly overtake me, and probably beat me to the finish line. If I grabbed all the juice and threw away what I didn't drink, Terry might fade in the final two miles.

Friendship won out. "Give the rest to Terry," I shouted to Mimi as I grabbed the cup of the thick mixture, which she held out for me.

Mimi understood, and quickly poured a second cup of my secret formula. She held it out as Terry approached. Worn down by the heat, he just pointed at his face. Mimi shook her head. Thinking it was water, Terry shouted, "In my face, throw it in my face." With no time left for explanations, Mimi shrugged, and tossed the contents of the cup into Aldrich's face as he ran past.

Several minutes later, as I waited in the recovery area, I couldn't understand why Terry hadn't blasted past in the final mile. As he staggered through the finish line, his hair was plastered to his forehead and he squinted through eyelids glued together with honey.

It was a great reminder that sportsmanship really does pay off.

Celebrate Winter

Victory in the Sauna

In 1970, the Biathlon World Championships were held in Östersund, Sweden. Sven Johanson, the legendary coach of the U.S. Biathlon Training Center in Alaska, was proud to lead a group of young American athletes back to his homeland.

The Swedes rival the Finns in their national passion for the sauna bath. As the championships drew near, Sven took us to the village of Umeå for a final training race. The competition was hosted by a local club, and following the award ceremony, we were invited to their sports center for a sauna.

This was not the warm room and swimming pool type of sauna that Americans find at a Holiday Inn. This was the authentic variety: a small cedar-lined room, heated to well over 100 degrees centigrade, (that's 212 degrees Fahrenheit), and a dipping pool that literally had ice floating on the surface.

At one point four Americans, including Sven, occupied the uppermost and therefore hottest bench. As we hunkered down near the ceiling, hanging our heads in the intense heat, three young Swedes entered the sauna. They recognized us as Americans, and with some reluctance, sat on the bench below us. It was embarrassing for them, masters at this form of bathing, to be seated on the lower, cooler level, while the visiting Americans, bumbling amateurs at the art of the sauna, quietly endured the intense heat inches from the ceiling.

We had been ready to leave when the young Swedes entered, but national pride demanded we wait a reasonable interval before exiting to the ice water pool. We suffered in silence, none of us wanting to be the first to give in.

The Swedes broke the spell by mumbling among themselves. On the top bench, as Sven listened, his muscles tensed. The Swedish racers had not recognized Sven, and had no way of knowing that he understood their every word. In English, he casually whispered to us, "Dey goin' try to force us out, boys! Don't nobody move tils I tell you."

The Swede closest to the door reached for the water bucket and casually ladled a couple of pints onto the red hot rocks. The droplets danced for an instant before they billowed toward the ceiling in a cloud of steam. The vapor caught me as I began to inhale, and I stopped, mid-breath. The scalding air curled the hair in my nostrils! My arms and back prickled. We were being poached alive!

But nobody moved. Slowly the steam subsided. As the cloud dissolved, it revealed the same Swede, ladling *more* water on the rocks. The steam billowed and I braced myself for another onslaught. About half the bucket of water remained, when the young Swede for a third time reached for the ladle. Sven sprang to the floor like a cat. He grabbed the bucket from the Swede, and turning toward the stove, he shouted, "Dammit boys, don't tease us; if you goin' heat 'dis place up, den heat it up good!" And he emptied the bucket on the stove.

Never have I seen three men move so quickly. The instant before the scalding vapor engulfed us, it was just elbows and buttocks clamoring for the exit. As the door slammed behind the Swedes, Sven ordered us to hit the deck. Four Americans dove for the floor, faces pressed to the cedar slats, gasping for breath.

Miraculously, we survived! The cloud began to dissipate, and Sven hauled us back to the top bench. With heads spinning and nostrils burning, we acted disinterested when wide-eyed faces peered through the glass in the door.

After a polite interval, we climbed down on jellied legs and tottered from the hot room. The three young bucks stood naked in the locker room, gaping at us. Normally the icy plunge is a challenge, even after the hottest sauna, but this time it was heaven. We paddled around, bobbed below the surface, and chatted lightheartedly.

When we finally made our way back to the locker room, every eye in the place followed us. We must have been quite a sight: wrinkled red skin hanging on exhausted, trembling frames. Yet there is a certain pleasure to beating someone at their own game.

John Caldwell's Wild West Tour

My early cross-country ski racing career benefited from the guidance of John Caldwell, Putney School's well-known math teacher and ski coach. After the publication of his famous *Cross-Country Ski Book* in 1964, Caldwell became the guru of the sport here in America, and Olympic hopefuls migrated from across the country to train in Putney, Vermont. Part of Caldwell's magic was his easy-going, fun-loving attitude toward training.

Even back in the days of wooden skis and knicker socks, everyone recognized that cross-country racers had to be in peak physical condition to be successful internationally. But Caldwell had a unique ability to make even the most demanding training sessions seem fun. Soccer was one of his favorite workouts. John would find a pasture at least twice the size of a regulation soccer field and mark out tiny goals, ensuring that there would be plenty of running and no long shots. Then he'd pick the teams, usually easterners versus the "cowboys" from out west, or the cross-country skiers against the jumpers — any natural rivalry that would insure a spirited contest. Finally, he'd announce, "No out of bounds, and no time outs!" Those games usually went until well after dark.

Another favorite John Caldwell workout was presented as "Downhill Practice." He would carefully explain that American cross-country skiers were losing time to their European rivals by being timid on the downhills. So he would stake out a slalom course on an infamous hillside pasture in Putney, and we'd run it again and again. He'd watch from the bottom and offer cryptic comments, "Not bad, now scoot back up there and try it again." Of course even the dumbest among us would soon realize it wasn't "Downhill Practice" at all, but Caldwell knew we would never have approached the workout with the same enthusiasm if he had more accurately described an afternoon of uphill sprints.

But John's classic workout was "The Tour." This was an endurance session that seldom had a planned route and never had a predetermined duration. More than just workouts, these were adventures, or expeditions. Often, when the location was Putney, Caldwell would lead his group of eager, national team members over the rolling hills, through the apple orchards, and deep into magnificent hardwood forests. Then he would disappear. Even in the winter, breaking trail through unbroken powder or scampering across an icy crust, the crafty coach would somehow double back on his own tracks, leaving his mystified racers to find their way back to Putney by trial and error. More than once, exhausted skiers from the Rockies or Alaska hitch-hiked back to Putney from the neighboring towns of Dummerston, Townsend, or even Westminster.

John Caldwell's most memorable ski tour took place in Yellowstone National Park. In the late autumn of 1971, prior to the tryouts for the Sapporo Winter Olympics, national team members, including cross-country skiers, Nordic combined competitors, and biathletes, had been invited to take advantage of the early season snow at Big Sky, Montana, a resort under development by the retired newscaster, Chet Huntley. The accommodations were great, there was plenty of snow, and the training was terrific.

But Big Sky was isolated. By Thanksgiving, after weeks of intense training and hundreds of kilometers on skis, the high-strung Olympic hopefuls were climbing the walls. So Caldwell, at the time head coach of the U.S. Cross-Country Team, planned a diversion.

On Thanksgiving Day, he loaded up four rugged Jeep Wagoneers with anyone who was "up for an adventure," and headed south through the beautiful Gallatin Canyon. More than an hour later we reached the village of West Yellowstone, the western entrance to the nation's first national park. Both the town and the imposing park entrance were totally deserted. Barriers blocked the access road and several signs made it clear that the park was closed for the season. Caldwell left the lead vehicle and checked at the ranger station. Then he walked through the trees to what appeared to be an office building. After several minutes, he returned and conferred with the other coaches. With a "what the hell" attitude, they shifted the Wagoneers into four-wheel-drive and plowed through a roadside snowbank, around the barricades and into the Park.

Then the fun really began! Coaches are just frustrated competitors, so immediately a race developed down the snow-packed, 14-mile road to Madison

Junction. Certain that there was no other traffic, and encouraged by the athletes, the coaches put those Jeeps through a deep-snow, four-wheel-drive, high-speed chase unlike anything they had ever experienced on a factory test track.

The thrill of racing down the snow-packed road inspired our next adventure, skijoring. Someone had brought a length of rope, so we took turns whipping over the snow-covered road on our delicate cross-country skis, pulled by the Jeeps, at 40 miles an hour. It was an unforgettable thrill.

We stopped several times to photograph animals: elk, bison, swans, geese, and even a coyote. Of course, having cross-country skis allowed the more determined photographers on the team to test their courage by getting up close and personal with their wildlife subjects.

One of the westerners in the group had been in the park before and led us to a spot where a boiling thermal spring overflowed into an icy river. We stripped down in the snow and gingerly found a narrow band of steaming water where the temperature was hot, but not scalding. A dozen exhausted athletes sat on the warm rocks, up to our chins in the strong current, luxuriating in nature's original Jacuzzi. Someone handed each of us an ice-cold beer. After several weeks of two and even three workouts a day, compounded by the unrelenting anxiety associated with trying to earn a spot on the Olympic team, that soak in the hot spring was absolute heaven.

Bright red and steaming, we fumbled back into our clothes and returned to the Jeeps. The coaches plowed on to Old Faithful. We parked in front of the magnificent wooden lodge and waited for the geyser's hourly eruption. I vaguely remember Caldwell engaged in an animated conversation with a park ranger, who must have been the winter caretaker of the lodge, but then Old Faithful erupted, and we watched with rapt attention. When Mother Nature's most reliable marvel sputtered to its conclusion, we loaded the Wagoneers and followed our tracks back to West Yellowstone. Tired and totally relaxed from our dip in the hot spring, most of us slept until we reached the park entrance.

I awoke to see the exit blocked by two Park Service vehicles, complete with flashing headlights and rotating beacons. Several armed park rangers, looking very official under their "Smoky the Bear" hats, stood in front of the roadblock. As Caldwell stepped out of the Jeep to "straighten things out," we rolled down the windows to hear what promised to be an entertaining exchange. John began amicably by explaining to the rangers that we had stopped on our way in to get permission, but that no one was around, and so on.... I heard him throw in the phrase "Olympic team" several times. The rangers gave no indication that they heard a word of Caldwell's explanation. They simply glared at him until he was finished.

Then the fireworks began. These dedicated public servants took their jobs, and their park, very seriously. The head ranger read Caldwell the riot act, enumerating in detail the federal infractions we had committed, including (but not limited to): illegally entering a national park, speeding on an unmaintained road, harassing the wildlife, indecent exposure, and consumption of alcohol in a restricted area. He concluded that we had committed violations that could easily result in $24,000 in federal fines, and possibly time in jail! It was the only time I ever remember John Caldwell at a loss for words.

He recovered enough to convince the rangers to let him get his athletes back to Big Sky, before returning to Yellowstone himself to straighten the mess out. It was a very quiet ride north, partly because we were so tired, but mostly because we were convinced that something serious would result from our carelessness. Somehow, Caldwell smoothed it all over. None of us had to appear in court or even chip in for the fines.

John Caldwell is still admired and respected by a couple of generations of American cross-country skiers. His original *Cross-Country Ski Book* has been reprinted eight times and has sold more than 500,000 copies. Because of his experience and his knowledge, he has represented the U.S. on several international Nordic skiing committees. But I suppose there are a couple of park rangers in West Yellowstone, Montana, who still have their doubts about him, even after almost fifty years.

Sapporo, 1972

Upon returning home from Vietnam I was reunited with my former teammates at the Biathlon Training Center in Alaska. Though we were all friends, we also competed at everything, so at this point our interactions contained an undercurrent of tension. The Sapporo Winter Olympics was only eight months away and only six of the twenty of us would make the team. I had been absent a year and had missed the previous winter's European trip, and some of my teammates had written me off. My return to Alaska and my determination to make the Sapporo team had upended their calculations.

During my absence there had been administrative turmoil on the team. Since 1961, the coach of the army's Biathlon Training Center was a Swedish immigrant to the U.S. named Sven Johanson. Sven was a remarkable athlete, having at one time been the Swedish National Champion in four different sports. He was also a no-nonsense coach who believed that hard training was the key to success. According to Sven, mental toughness was critical in biathlon, and he had little patience for athletes who complained of fatigue, illness or injury. One of Sven's former athletes was Jay Bowerman of Eugene, Oregon, the son of the famous and innovative University of Oregon track coach, Bill Bowerman. Having grown up listening to some of the most cutting-edge training concepts of the time, Jay felt (and others agreed) that U.S. biathletes would never succeed internationally under Sven's antiquated coaching, but since he was a government employee, it would not be easy to replace him. The coach for the Sapporo Olympic biathlon team, however, was an appointment, and it was relatively easy for Sven's detractors to have someone else named to that position (even though Sven had coached the previous two Olympic teams and all the athletes in contention to make the '72 team). Since Sven was self-conscious about his command of written English, upon my return from Vietnam I was recruited to write letters in Sven's defense, which not only failed but put me at odds with his replacement.

The 1972 Olympic biathlon trials were held in Jackson, Wyoming, and were fraught with challenges. Altitude, or elevation above sea level, plays a role in any endurance sport, and it can be especially significant in biathlon, where the transition from vigorous, heart-pounding exertion to steady, poised marksman occurs in seconds. The team would be selected by the best three out of four tryout events. Since the two competitions in Sapporo were to be a 20-kilometer individual and a 4x7.5-kilometer relay, two of the tryout events were 20 kilometers, and the remaining two were 7.5 kilometers to simulate the relay distance. The weather didn't cooperate. Prior to the first competition, an overnight blizzard forced the postponement of the race. The storms persisted and the first event was postponed three times.

In the 20-kilometer event back then, we shot on paper targets 150 meters from the firing line. Before the start of the race, athletes would "zero their rifles" by shooting a three-round group. The rifle coach, studying the group through a powerful spotting scope, might recommend a correction to the athlete, who would turn small adjustment knobs on his rifle sight to center the group. Unless there were severe weather conditions — strong wind, blowing snow or bright sun — sight adjustments were usually minor, seldom more than a couple of clicks of the adjustment knob. Most of us had a "normal zero" on our sights, indicated by a small stripe of bright red nail polish. Rules prohibit shooting coaches from communicating sight corrections to the athletes on the shooting range, although information can be radioed to other coaches out on the course. During tryout races, coaches are supposed to remain neutral, treating all competitors equitably.

When the storms finally broke and the first tryout race took place, I finished with some optimism. Having passed a number of other racers on the course, I knew I had skied well. But my heart sank as I approached our shooting coach and he simply asked to see my rifle. He carefully inspected the sights then explained that all twenty of my shots were grouped at nine o'clock, to the left of the bull's eye. He quizzed me about the sight adjustment I had made during the pre-race zeroing period.

Eventually, we determined that at some point prior to the start, when I had put my rifle down to test my skis or remove my warmups, someone had turned the windage knob on my sights one complete revolution, so that the nail polish line appeared as it did following zeroing. There was no way to determine who might have sabotaged my race, and I never found out. I did learn, however, not to let my rifle out of my sight for the remainder of the tryout series, and that all of the three remaining races had to count. The stress and anxiety continued through the final event, held in heavy wet snow, just at the freezing point. Before the skating era, when all cross-country skiing consisted of classic, kick and glide technique, new snow at the freezing point was a nightmare for waxing. Select a wax slightly too warm for the snow conditions and thick, heavy chunks of snow would adhere to the bases, making gliding impossible. Select a wax too cold for the conditions, and your skis would have no kick in the glazed tracks. Although both conditions were equally frustrating to competitors, the final tryout race illustrated that slick skis were better than icing up, since most of the athletes early in the start order iced up and finished well behind in the results, and all the top finishers started in the second half of the start list.

When the dust (actually, heavy, wet snow) settled, the 1972 Olympic biathlon team consisted of two members of the training center at Fort Richardson, two recent veterans of the center, and two old-timers who had been out of the service for several years. Several legitimate contenders were sidelined by illness or bad luck, while at least three who had been given little chance of making the team, were successful. I was one of those three. Because of the weather delays and postponements, within hours of the final race we were packed and driving from Jackson to Denver where the Olympic team was being outfitted. Since biathlon was at that time such an obscure sport in the U.S., it was tremendously exciting to be part of the much larger, Winter Olympic team, which included prominent Alpine skiers, figure skaters and others. In addition to what seemed like endless paperwork and presentations, the outfitting of the Olympic team consisted primarily of issuing an astounding amount of official clothing.

Prior to every Olympic Games, the U.S. Olympic Committee welcomes bids from clothing manufacturers to outfit the team, in exchange for the priceless publicity of the worldwide television coverage, especially of the opening ceremony. In 1972 the U.S Olympic team's clothing supplier was Sears and Roebuck, and they spared no expense. While much of the casual clothes provided to the athletes might have been available in Sears' stores nationwide, the parade uniforms (long, blue leather coats, distinctive cowboy hats and tall, fur-trimmed, leather boots) were custom-made for the Games. We received so much clothing that we were also provided cardboard boxes in which to mail most of it home.

The U.S. team to the Sapporo Winter Olympics flew from Denver to Tokyo on two chartered, Pan American jets. An hour into the flight, our pilot came onto the intercom to let us know that each of the air traffic control stations that were tracking our flight across the western U.S. knew we were the Olympic team and wished us good luck. Several hours later, when we landed in Tokyo for an overnight, I vividly remember deplaning next to a huge, ominous jetliner emblazoned with the hammer and sickle of the Soviet Union. The next day we flew on to Sapporo, which looked strangely familiar, since missionaries from New England helped to establish the city a century earlier, and many of the historical buildings could have been in Portsmouth, Concord or Burlington. The Olympic Village consisted of a couple of multistory apartment buildings overlooking a central commons that housed four distinct cafeterias (Asian, North American, northern European, and Mediterranean foods). The North American cafeteria was popular for its cheeseburgers and french fries, while the Mediterranean dining room was crowded in the evenings because the French and Italians brought their own wine.

The Olympic Village was linked to downtown Sapporo by a brand-new commuter train. Rather than concentrate all the Olympic venues in one location, the planners had elected to build the sports facilities in neighborhoods across the city. With our Olympic credentials we could ride the train or catch a bus to watch a hockey practice or speed-skating training in a remote corner of Sapporo. In fact, as arguably the most obscure and least understood athletes at the Games, a couple of us discovered the ironic pleasure of riding the bus with the figure skaters to their evening practice. We chatted with medal contenders like JoJo Starbuck, Ken Shelley and Janet Lynn, then watched with interest as they practiced their jumps, spins and lifts.

The opening ceremony was a kaleidoscope of colorful and poignant images. For all the effort and expense Sears invested in the parade uniforms, someone neglected to remind the designers that it was the WINTER Olympics. As the U.S. delegation marched into the stadium, across the ice of the speed-skating oval, the slick leather soles of our pilgrim boots provided no grip at all, and we struggled to stay upright. Several members of the U.S. delegation fell, a few were injured (fortunately, we learned later, the injured were U.S. Olympic officials rather than athletes). We probably appeared to be hung-over sailors, not the image Sears was hoping for. The opening ceremony was poignant and beautiful with children, doves, balloons and, of course, the Olympic flame. I was struck by the fact that less than thirty years after World War II, Emperor Hirohito was sitting across the ice from me in the VIP box, welcoming the world to Japan with the opening of the Olympic Games.

Typically, one of the first events of the Winter Olympics is the Nordic combined, a competition on the 70-meter ski jump, followed the next day by a pursuit-start, 15-kilometer cross-country ski race where the winner of the jump is chased, at calculated intervals, by the other competitors. The event was established by Norwegians to recognize the best overall skier, and has been dominated by Scandinavians and Central Europeans. But in Sapporo, a teenager named Hideki Nakano electrified the host country by winning the jump. He became an instant celebrity and a national hero. Unfortunately, the pressure probably got to him and he finished last in the cross-country the next day.

We trained at the biathlon venue to become familiar with the ski course and the idiosyncrasies of the shooting range. Some of the workouts were time trials in which I improved my results from Jackson. As the day of the 20-kilometer individual biathlon event approached, I anticipated a team meeting where the coach and team leader would announce the four of us who would be competing, and assignments for the other two athletes in support and logistical details. Instead, I noticed the start list for the event posted on a bulletin board outside the dining hall, and I was not one of the four Americans entered. I was shocked and confused, since I had clearly earned one of the starting spots in the 20 kilometer. I considered approaching the coach and team leader, but hesitated for one reason. For several years prior to Sapporo the strategy had been to focus on a strong relay performance. I had been a part of that plan until my tour in Vietnam. Unfortunately, I had not been able to clearly demonstrate my ability to be on that relay team at the tryouts in Jackson, although the time trials on the Sapporo course had been encouraging. Perhaps, I thought, the coaches were planning a switch, entering my teammate in the individual event, and racing me in the relay. If that was the plan, I was willing to bite my tongue and sit out the 20 kilometer. On the day of the first Sapporo Olympic biathlon event, I was at a remote part of the course handing bottles of energy drink to my four teammates as they raced past. It turned out to be an encouraging effort: Pete Karns finished fourteenth, tying the best-ever Olympic finish for an American biathlete.

For a change of scenery, a few of us decided to have dinner in the northern European cafeteria. After getting our meals, we approached a large table occupied by only one athlete. We asked if we could join him and he nodded his approval. Soon after we sat down, a TV crew with camera and microphone on an extended boom surrounded our tablemate. While he attempted to finish his meal, they repeatedly stuck the microphone in his face. Finally, the pestered athlete took his knife and loudly rapped his drinking glass, causing the sound man to retract the mic and tear off his headphones. Defeated, the film crew left the dining room. It was then we realized that our tablemate was speed skater Ard Shenk from the Netherlands, who would win three gold medals in Sapporo.

At some point during the Games, the international governing body for biathlon hosted a reception for athletes, officials and VIPs. I remember two conversations. At previous competitions I had made friends with Malcolm Hurst, one of the top biathletes from Great Britain. Like us, most of the Brits were in the military. They had a Norwegian coach and spent much of the off-season on temporary duty, training in Scandinavia. After the typical, casual conversation at the reception, Hurst and I realized that we both had missed the previous competitive season, he on duty in Northern Ireland and me in Vietnam. As we shared experiences, a couple of commonalities emerged. We both had misgivings about the conflicts in which we had served. With dark humor, Malcolm described his mission in Northern Ireland as "being a target for both sides." Another observation we agreed on was that it was far better to compete peacefully with skis and rifles than to carry a rifle in combat. We wondered whether that might be a subtle reason why international biathletes are typically friendly and even helpful to each other. Many if not most biathletes have been part of their nation's military, and at least in training, if not in actual combat, have experienced the chaos and trauma of armed conflict. Many understand how much better it is to shoot at targets rather than at each other.

The second conversation was with Alexander Tikhonov, emerging young superstar of the dominant biathlon team from the Soviet Union. I had met Tikhonov four years earlier at the 1969 Biathlon World Championships in Zakopane, Poland, where he had won the 20-kilometer event. While most of the Soviet athletes were reserved and unapproachable, Tikhonov was gregarious, even brash. Like many of the Soviet athletes, he was an avid pin-trader. At most major international sports events, athletes, officials and spectators eagerly trade commemorative lapel pins. Tikhonov approached me in Zakopane, opened his winter coat to display an astounding array of pins affixed to the lining, and asked, "You change?" I had a small assortment of U.S. biathlon pins, which at the time were rare in Europe, so he was interested. In 1969 the Soviets were still the enemy and the hammer and sickle was still a very ominous symbol to Americans, so when we agreed on a pin exchange, I upped the ante by suggesting we trade racing shirts. Mine was white with a red, white and blue U.S. biathlon shoulder patch, his was Soviet red with a hammer and sickle patch. He surprised me by accepting, and I thoroughly impressed my teammates by scoring a Soviet racing jersey.

Tikhonov and I renewed our friendship the next year at the Biathlon World Championships in Ostersund, Sweden. He expressed great interest in the Scott, aluminum ski poles we had been provided, and I was interested in the Russian carrying harness used on the rifles of all the Soviet bloc athletes. We made the trade and the friendship flourished. When I saw Tikhonov at the reception in Sapporo, he embraced me and announced to everyone, "Morton John, mya druug" — in Russian, "my brother."

I discovered the starting order for the biathlon relay from the same bulletin board outside the dining hall, and again my name wasn't listed. This time I did ask the team leader for a meeting, where the coach who had replaced Sven made it clear that they were "free to select whomever they saw fit to race, and furthermore, I had been a troublemaker since my return from Vietnam." It was immediately clear that there would be no reasoning with them, so I left the meeting resigned to my role of being a spectator at Sapporo.

The day of the biathlon relay was an emotional roller coaster since my four teammates who competed did remarkably well. They were in third place for the first thirty minutes of the race, slipping to fourth for the second thirty minutes. They ultimately finished in sixth place of the thirteen teams competing, good enough for an Olympic certificate. While I felt a sense of pride in the team's impressive result, it was heart-wrenching not to have had the opportunity to compete.

As expected, the Soviets won the biathlon relay, as they had since 1969, but their victory had not been assured. Tikhonov, their leadoff skier, put them in a deep hole by missing five shots, standing. Fortunately, two of his older, more experienced teammates, Rinnat Safin and Viktor Mamatov, saved the day for the Soviets by shooting clean and retaking the lead. That evening in the Mediterranean cafeteria, Safin and Mamatov, wearing their gold medals and perhaps fueled by some Italian wine or Russian vodka, were celebrating boisterously, somewhat unusual for the typically reserved, disciplined Soviets. An unsettling spinoff occurred the next day. One of my teammates wanted a Russian carrying harness for his rifle and had Scott ski poles to trade. I offered to take him to the Soviet team's accommodations to facilitate the deal. We displayed our credentials to the burley Russian guard at the entrance, who showed no intention of admitting us until I mentioned we were visiting Alexander Tikhonov. As we approached Tikhonov's room on one of the upper floors, we heard harsh shouting through a partially opened door. A stealthy glance into the room revealed Safin and Mamatov standing at attention in front of Tikhonov, who was shouting at them as he repeatedly slapped their faces. We retreated quickly without being seen.

Before the end of the Games, I encountered Mamatov, and congratulated him on his impressive, come-from-behind victory in the relay. He was subdued in his reply. I knew that many of the Europeans, especially the Communist Bloc athletes, were anticipating the 1973 Biathlon World Championships to be hosted in Lake Placid, New York. I casually remarked that I'd look forward to seeing him in Lake Placid the next winter. Stoically holding back his emotions, he responded, "I never see America."

"But Viktor, you're their best. You saved the relay for them."

Mamatov just shook his head and walked away. A year later, when the Soviet team arrived in Lake Placid, Viktor Mamatov was not among them.

As we packed our skis, rifles and clothing for the long trip home, the skies opened with torrential rain. Riding to the airport, I remember flooded streets and parked cars submerged by the wake of our bus. Behind me, a coach put his hand to his mouth before retching violently out the window. I eventually realized he was removing his dentures before vomiting the previous night's celebration. On the chartered flight back to the States, I sat across the aisle from an Alpine ski coach who drank his way across the Pacific while aggressively flirting with one of his female athletes. We stopped in Seattle to go through Customs and to off-load the West Coast athletes. We flew on to Chicago, where the local Olympic fans provided an impressive welcome for gold medal speed skaters Dianne Holum and Anne Henning. The flight continued on to New York, where the rest of us disembarked. A couple of us biathletes, who were still active duty military, were headed directly to Beirut, Lebanon, for the CISM Military Ski Championships. After another brief outfitting process and checking of passports and rifle permits, one of my friends from the Unit in Alaska, who had just missed the Olympic team but would be participating in the upcoming CISM Games, shared an observation. He had been instructed to travel to George Wilson's office in Washington, DC, to pick up the international rifle permits for the U. S. athletes headed to Beirut. While waiting in Wilson's office for the permits, he overheard a conversation between Wilson and the Olympic coach (who had replaced Sven), during which the coach assured Wilson that Morton had not raced in Sapporo.

Memories of Beirut

Late in February 1972, the World Military Ski Championships (organized annually by NATO's Counseil International du Sport Militaire, commonly referred to as the CISM Games) were hosted at The Cedars, high in the snowcapped mountains east of Beirut. It was an epic adventure from the beginning. A couple of us who had been members of the Olympic Biathlon Team in Sapporo could have cut our air miles (and jet lag) by more than 50 percent by flying west from Japan across China to Lebanon. But that year the U.S. Olympians returned from the Olympic Games on charter flights that stopped in Anchorage, Seattle and Chicago.

For those of us competing at CISM, we flew on to New York, London, Rome, Istanbul, and finally, Beirut. Not only were we exhausted from the stress of the Olympics and airline flights around two-thirds of the globe, but the Beirut International Airport seemed like a military stronghold. Guards in camouflage fatigues with submachine guns slung over their shoulders carefully scrutinized the arriving passengers. Outside, the sunbaked runways were protected by endless coils of concertina wire and ominous, antiaircraft gun emplacements.

We were met by a young Lebanese Air Force lieutenant who would be our team's guide and interpreter during the CISM Games. After gathering our skis, rifles and baggage, we loaded a couple of mini vans for the drive to The Cedars. Our route took us through Beirut, north along the Mediterranean, and finally, east into the mountains. Although the countryside was warm and dry near the coast, after miles of harrowing switchbacks, we arrived in a high mountain valley, buried by a couple of feet of heavy, spring snow. Primitive ski lifts reached up toward the peaks, while European-style chalets clustered near the base. There were no trees except for a small grove of ancient cedars, all that remains of the legendary forest that provided timbers for the Phoenician's ships and beams for King Solomon's temple more than two thousand years ago.

Our accommodations were spartan, perhaps because soldiers are expected to rough it, but more likely because it was the best our hosts could provide.

The meals were a stark contrast to the lavish variety provided at the Sapporo Olympic Village. In Lebanon, we survived on Mediterranean flatbread and warm Coca Cola, which our hosts served breakfast, lunch, and dinner.

The competitions provided an additional level of challenge. Since the snow was old, the nights were cold, and the temperatures rose well above freezing during the day, we were training and racing on either bulletproof crust or slush. This was well before the advent of the skating technique, so waxing was a nightmare. It was not unusual to rocket down icy tracks on blue klister in the mountain's shadow, emerge into the blinding sunlight where the wet snow grabbed your skis like mashed potatoes, and then fight frantically to stay upright through the craters created by previous racers.

But far more memorable than the minor organizational shortcomings was the hospitality and friendliness of the people. One of the events was a cross-country relay, and the Lebanese military was represented by Najem Najem, Roget Kasab, and Alli Achtin. Never have I seen Nordic skiers fall and laugh with such abandon. Only once did they scowl in genuine anger, when a fighter jet skimmed the ridgetop and roared over our heads, down the valley. I recognized it as an F-4 Phantom and assumed it was one of ours, stationed in Turkey. Through the interpreter, we learned that it was an Israeli jet intentionally embarrassing the Lebanese during their military championships. When the competitions ended, our hosts showed us the sights of Beirut and arranged a day trip to Baalbek, the famous Roman ruins in the Bekaa Valley near the Syrian border.

I hadn't thought much about Lebanon until the conflict of 1982 erupted and newspapers began to print photos of the destruction in Beirut, where the Bekaa Valley was described as a Hezbollah stronghold. Now I think often of the Lebanese soldiers with whom I skied and laughed in the winter of 1972. I wonder if they survived Lebanon's bloody civil war in '75–'76, invasions by Syria in the early '80s and repeated Israeli air strikes into the mid-'90s. I think of how different our experiences must have been over the past decades, and what a strange, dreamlike memory that week of skiing must be for men who have spent most of their lives swept up in violent, bloody conflict.

Innsbruck, 1976

The 1976 Innsbruck Winter Olympic team was outfitted in New York City. We stayed in the Statler Hotel, across the street from Grand Central Station. For those of us who had been living and training in Alaska, New York City was quite a culture shock. It was winter and I remember feeling very conflicted about the abundance of clothing we were being given while every time we exited the hotel we passed homeless people trying to stay warm, huddled on the steel grates in the sidewalk that vented the subway below. I was also shocked that in one of the largest and most famous hotels in the city, the desk clerk repeatedly warned us to keep all three locks on our rooms bolted. We thought he was just overcautious until we were awakened in the middle of the night by the rattling of the locks and the door cracking open. My teammate responded quickly, "Come on in you idiot. You just broke into the room of two Olympic shooters, each with a Remington .223." The door slammed shut and we eventually got back to sleep.

Since I had known for some time that this would be my last international trip as a U.S. biathlete, I had given some thought to finding a meaningful gift for my Soviet friend, Alexander Tikhonov. We had met in 1969 when the Cold War was still in full swing. In spite of the language barrier, we communicated with a bit of German and hand gestures. While most of the Russian athletes and coaches were reserved and seemed to avoid us, Tikhonov eagerly traded pins, sporting equipment and even clothing. My wife knit him a ski hat that he wore in competition for several years, referring to it as "mya talisman." At the 1973 Biathlon World Championships, hosted in Lake Placid, New York, I went to Tikhonov's hotel room to say good-bye. He greeted me with, "John, klien problem!" Pointing to his partially filled, large suitcase, he made me understand that while he still had plenty of space for blue jeans and LP record albums, he was out of money. I opened my wallet and gave him all the cash I had (which was less than $100). He was moved by the gesture and handed back

$10 so that I wasn't completely broke. Then, with a crushing bear hug he said, "Next year, Minsk, John, all team USA, no problem!"

True to his word, the following winter when we arrived in Minsk, Belorussia, for the 1974 Biathlon World Championships, he met our plane and whisked me off in his private car. Rather than going to the hotel with my teammates, Tikhonov took me to an impressive store featuring characteristic Russian handicrafts. "John, how many in USA delegation?" he asked. I tallied the athletes and coaches and responded with ten fingers plus two. "Twelve, Alexander, we have twelve from the USA." Then he strode around the shop pointing to various items: nesting dolls, carved wooden boxes, brightly colored woven shawls, intricately painted wooden plates. At each stop, he'd look at me and ask, "Harasho, good?" I'd smile, nod and mumble, "Yes, Alexander, very nice," and he'd command the shopkeeper to wrap up twelve of them. We left the shop with so much loot, it took two trips to get it all to his car. We caught up with the rest of the U.S. team at the hotel and Tikhonov was like Santa Claus distributing gifts to all the athletes and coaches from the USA.

So, anticipating that '76 would be my final trip as an athlete, at the previous World Championships I had asked Tikhonov what he would like from America. He thought for a moment and then responded, "Winchester hunting rifle, very good, better than any Soviet." Since by that time Tikhonov had become friendly with several Americans, we chipped in and bought him a Winchester 30.06, one of the most popular hunting rifles in North America. As a bonus, we added a beautiful, Leopold scope, and of course, plenty of ammunition. While in New York for the Olympic processing, I had the idea that it would be extra special to affix a brass plate to the stock, commemorating the gift. What would probably have been impossible anywhere else, just took some leg work in New York. First, I located a newspaper that was printed in Russian. What I thought would be a simple request turned out to be more complicated, since the folks who produced the newspaper were fiercely anti-communist and were not inclined to help me. Eventually, I convinced one of them to print in Cyrillic script, "To Alexander Tikhonov, a true champion and international sportsman, from his friends on the U.S. Biathlon Team, presented at the 1976 Innsbruck Olympic Games."

Next, I found a jewelry store that could engrave the inscription onto a brass plate overnight. On the day we left for Innsbruck, I picked up the engraved plate, attached it to the rifle, and locked the Winchester in my rifle box along with my biathlon Remington.

Like many Winter Olympic venues, the city of Innsbruck, Austria, was the site for most of the events, while biathlon, cross-country and Nordic combined were held in the scenic Alpine village of Seefeld, almost an hour's drive to the northwest. This was both a curse and a blessing. Innsbruck was a city in the river valley; Seefeld was an exclusive resort, high in the Alps. While all the glamor sports operated out of the Innsbruck Olympic Village (Alpine skiing, figure skating, ice hockey, ski jumping and speed skating) and were the focus of the media, up in Seefeld we stayed in posh hotels and walked to our competition venues. It appeared that only a handful of extremely dedicated journalists from Scandinavia had discovered where we were training and competing.

The major attraction in Seefeld (aside from the Olympic Nordic skiing courses) was a wonderful new spa constructed for the Olympics but clearly intended to be a tourist amenity for years to come. It featured a heated swimming pool partially within the impressive stone-and-glass building and partially outside, under the stars. For the Olympic athletes, the major attractions were the saunas, one for men, another for women and a third open to everyone. Within a couple of days, all of the Olympic athletes had discovered the Seefeld saunas and the co-ed sauna was by far the most popular. The hot rooms were really hot and just outside the door was a dipping pool with chunks of ice floating in the water. Eventually, our coaches restricted us from taking a sauna every day, although our biathlon team leader, a Finnish immigrant to the U.S., was addicted and eventually looked like his wrinkled skin was a couple of sizes too big for his body.

The day of the Opening Ceremony was always a mixed blessing, hours of "hurry up and wait" often standing in the cold, for a few moments of unforgettable inspiration marching into the arena as part of the U.S. delegation. The Innsbruck Opening Ceremony was held at the massive Bergisel Ski Jump, which dominated a hillside overlooking Innsbruck. As the ceremony finally got underway, a rumor spread through the assembled athletes that the Austrian Air Force had shot down a private plane that had violated the restricted airspace established around the event and had refused to change course. We were grateful to return to the relative obscurity of Seefeld once the Olympic flame had been ignited and the Games were officially underway.

The Nordic ski trails in Seefeld were typical of those throughout the Alps, relatively flat skiing through the open pastures of the valley floor combined with tough climbs and fast descents through the steep, forested walls of the valleys. The biathlon range was located adjacent to the start/finish area of the cross-country facility, and everything was a short walk (or ski) from the hotels and shops of the village. Before the competitions got underway, word spread among the athletes that a Finnish company, Exel, was promoting their innovative new carbon fiber ski poles by providing every Olympic skier a complementary pair. A couple of us found the rented chalet where the Exel reps were staying and were guided to the attached garage, where hundreds of pairs of poles were neatly lined up against a wall. The handles of the poles formed a consistent incline, from shortest to tallest, at least until the last sets of poles, which were several inches taller than the others. At the time, Finland's national hero was Juha Mieto, who was not only a multiple World Cup and Olympic medalist, but also stood 6 feet, 5 inches. As the Exel service rep was selecting poles for us, I pointed to the unusually tall ones at the end of the line. "You must have to make them specially for Mieto," I said. The rep smiled, pleased that I'd made the connection to their hero. "Yes, yes, those are for Mieto, specially made." It was a skillful marketing ploy by Exel, which since 1976 has been the dominant supplier of Nordic ski poles, worldwide.

The team leader for the biathletes from Great Britain was a crusty, aristocratic, retired general everyone addressed simply as "the

Brigadier." We shared a hotel with the Brits in Seefeld, and a few days into our stay I noticed an elegant, silver and green Bentley parked prominently in front of the hotel. My buddy on the British Team, Malcom Hurst, confirmed that the Bentley belonged to the Brigadier, who had it shipped over from England for the Games. A couple of us thought a little good-natured prank might help defuse the precompetition stress, so late one night, armed with several rolls of white athletic tape, on the spacious expanse of the Bentley's front doors we wrote:

British Biathlon Team Bus

Apparently, the Brigadier didn't have much of a sense of humor and the tape was immediately removed, but his athletes thought it was great.

The high point of the Innsbruck Olympics for many of us came early in the schedule of competitions. Typically, the men's 30-kilometer cross-country is one of the first Nordic events. We biathletes were finishing a combination workout (skiing and shooting) at the range when someone suggested we ski up to the cross-country stadium to see how the men's 30 kilometer was going. Wearing our USA warmups and our Olympic training bibs, with our rifles on our backs, we skied the short distance to the adjacent cross-country facility. In those days, security was virtually nonexistent and we found ourselves standing near the finish line, among the cross-country competitors and their coaches. A large, electronic scoreboard reflected the current standings: Saveliev, USSR, in first; Bill Koch, USA, second! Normally, the better skiers are seeded later in the start list, so we assumed that Kochie had had a tremendous race, but would surely be bumped down the list as the hotshots late in the start order arrived at the finish line. But as racers continued to collapse across the line, all the standings on the scoreboard changed except for first and second. Then, European coaches, noticing the USA on our warmups, approached, slapping us on the back and even hugging us, saying, "Beel Coke, okay! Very good! USA, very good!" We looked at each other in disbelief. Maybe his silver-medal performance would hold up. We held our breath in the following minutes until all the competitors had finished, and Koch-USA was still in second place! It was a remarkable

41

breakthrough for American Nordic skiers. Kochie had just proven it was possible to beat the Europeans at their game. Psychologically, he opened the door for all the rest of us.

That evening as several of us biathletes strolled through the village of Seefeld, we were mobbed by Austrian kids with their autograph books, all of them clambering, "Beel Coke, you Beel Coke?" Lyle Nelson, our top biathlete casually glanced at the rest of us and mouthed, "Why not? Let's make their day." So four obscure American biathletes spent almost an hour in downtown Seefeld signing "Bill Koch-USA" in hundreds of Austrian kids' autograph books.

There had been a virulent stomach flu going through Seefeld. It seemed to hit hard, vomiting and diarrhea, but it was over quickly. A couple of our guys got hit early, before the competitions began. The night before the individual 20 kilometer, I woke up sweating with a churning stomach. By morning, it was obvious I had the bug, and a teammate was selected to race in my place. We must have been really jinxed because he took a bad fall that broke the stock of his rifle, so it was impossible for him to complete the race. Meanwhile, I was spending most of my time in the water closet. Within a couple of days, we had experienced the euphoria of Kochie's silver medal and the intense discouragement of the biathlon 20 kilometer.

Fortunately, I began to recover quickly, but because I hadn't raced the 20 kilometer, the coaches weren't sure about who should race the biathlon relay. Ultimately, they decided to hold a time trail on the Olympic course to determine who would race. It was my second Winter Olympics, and I was faced with the distinct possibility that once again I wouldn't get to compete. Although I'd been hit hard by the stomach flu a few days earlier, I doubt I had ever been more motivated in a competition. I skied my brains out and shot well enough to earn a spot on the relay team. In fact, sadly (or ironically) during the actual Olympic biathlon relay on the very same course, I skied 25 seconds slower than I did in the time trial. We finished eleventh out of fifteen nations.

For many Olympians, perhaps most, while it is a tremendous honor to make the team and to compete for the USA, the greatest disappointment is to have not been able to do your best on the day when it really counted. I believe about 10 percent of Olympic participants win medals. For all the rest of us the goal is simply to "do your best." Some athletes achieve that goal by achieving a personal-best time in an event. But for many others, the stress, the media attention, illness or injury sabotages their effort to do their best when it really counts. For them, participation in the Olympic Games is a mixed blessing.

For most of us on the '76 Olympic biathlon team, the completion of the competitions was a relief. We took a van down to Innsbruck to have dinner at the Olympic Village and see a hockey game. I had an additional mission. A couple of years earlier, the U.S. cross-country ski team was competing in southern Germany when they met an American executive of BMW. The executive had invited the team to Munich to tour the factory and offered them the opportunity to buy BMW 2002 models for remarkably low, factory-discount prices. Contact had been renewed with the executive, and a similar factory tour had been arranged following the '76 Olympic Closing Ceremony. I had received word that the executive's daughter was an aspiring figure skater who idolized Dorothy Hamill. The new BMW 320i was the official car of the Winter Olympics and several of us had been drooling over them for the past two weeks. I was convinced if I could get Dorothy Hamill's autograph for the executive's daughter, it would guarantee us bargain-basement prices on a new car.

While my teammates headed for the cafeteria line, I scoured the Olympic athletes' dining room for America's Olympic sweetheart. Fortunately, I spotted her and even more fortunately when I approached her she didn't recoil in frustration. With a big smile she asked, "Is this for you?" I responded honestly that it was for the daughter of someone who was a huge fan of American figure skating. In seconds she wrote "With Love and Luck, Dorothy Hamill," and with a couple of deft strokes of the pen created the image of a twirling figure skater. I thanked her and a few days later watched with special interest as she won her gold medal.

Watching some figure skaters through the years, I found myself getting tense hoping they wouldn't fall and miss their chance for greatness, but Dorothy Hamill put everyone at ease with her performance. No one who watched her skate in Innsbruck had the slightest doubt that the gold medal was hers. A week or so later, several of us salivated as we spent three hours touring the BMW factory in Munich. Watching the cars be painted, I chose the color I wanted. At the end of the tour, the executive met our group and I presented him with Dorothy's autograph, which almost brought tears to his eyes. Then, suddenly, he was gone; there was no offer to buy discounted cars and we left the factory. I wish I'd kept the autograph.

The day we were scheduled to depart Seefeld, our team leader roused us out of bed early, announcing that he had arranged a friendly competition through his friends on the Finnish team. There would be a 5-kilometer relay race, Finland against the USA, on the Olympic women's cross-country course. Most of the Finnish participants were cross-country skiers while the Americans were all biathletes. I ended up skiing anchor for the USA, and as the race developed, I realized that I'd be going out against Helena Taklo, who had just won a gold and a silver (missing her second gold by a second). We started nearly together, and although she was working hard, I was able to keep up. We battled through the 5 kilometers onto the long, flat approach to the finish line. Striding side by side, I looked over at her and asked, "You want to tie for the sake of international friendship?" She looked at me like I had accused her of doping and picked up the pace. I found a gear I didn't know I had and beat her to the finish line to the cheers of my teammates and the satisfaction of my Finnish team leader (who probably had several bets riding on the "friendly relay"). When I attempted to approach Helena, she turned and walked away. The reason she was an Olympic champion was that she didn't like to lose, at anything.

To Survive or to Celebrate Winter, That Is the Question

I'll always be grateful to my mother for what some folks today would consider child abuse. One snowy winter day before I was ten, my sister and I were fighting over which television channel to watch when our mother lost her patience. "You kids watch too much TV! Get your clothes on and go play outside. Don't come back 'til lunch." A cruel woman!

We lived high on a windy hill, surrounded by cow pastures that were blanketed in snow. When it became apparent no amount of whining at the back door would soften our mother's resolve, my sister and I set about amusing ourselves in the snow. We built forts and dug snow caves. We went sliding and tobogganing. We skated with other kids on a nearby frog pond. At some point during that winter, our mom bought us secondhand skis, which for me, opened a whole new world of fun.

Since then, skiing has taken me all over the world to places where people celebrate winter. I've learned that enjoying winter has little to do with the weather conditions, the hours of daylight or the length of the season. It has much more to do with attitude. While many Americans dread the cold, dark days of winter, and others stoically try to make the best of it, there are places where people actually look forward to winter.

Our neighbors to the north in Canada are pros at celebrating winter. From Labrador to the Yukon, as soon as snow covers the ground, the festivals begin. In Quebec City there is the famous Winter Carnival with hair-raising toboggan runs, illuminated ice sculptures and the unbelievable lifeboat race across the ice-choked St. Lawrence River.

In Ottawa, a skating festival draws thousands to the frozen canals that thread through Canada's capital city. And at the other end of the country, in the tiny Native village of Inuvik, not far from the Arctic Ocean, they used to host the Top of the World Ski Championships, an international gathering of Nordic competitors who enjoyed mid-winter snow conditions in April. I watched the local kids in Inuvik enthusiastically chase a soccer ball across a snow-covered playground during a school recess, ski like little rockets around their cross-country trails after school got out, and then play ice hockey under the lights in the evening! Now that's far more than simply surviving winter.

In the late 1990s I had the opportunity to visit a new Alpine ski center in South Korea. In its third year of operation, the Muju Resort drew thirty thousand visitors a day on winter weekends. Only two resorts in America could boast attendance numbers like that. And at Muju, the visitors are not all skiers. On a beautifully groomed sledding hill, I watched hundreds of people, from toddlers to grandparents, squeal with delight as they raced down the slope on simple plastic sleds.

But probably the undisputed experts on celebrating winter are the Scandinavians. Who could doubt the Finn's devotion to winter when their national bathing ritual, the sauna, requires a plunge through the ice of a frozen lake, or a roll in the snow? And what about the way the Swedes celebrate Christmas: homes decorated with evergreens and blazing with candles, while the air inside is rich with the delicious aroma of their legendary smorgasbord.

Anyone who watched the television coverage of the Lillehammer Olympics saw a nation that truly relishes winter. Thousands of families in thick wool sweaters, waving flags and hauling their lunches in rucksacks, hiked the two miles from the train station to the Nordic skiing stadium, laughing and singing in the sub-zero cold. Hundreds of other Norwegians camped in tent villages along the race course to be assured a front row seat for the competitions. While American journalists complained about the bitter cold, Olympic athletes and vast crowds of devoted Norwegian skiing fans thanked heaven for ideal snow conditions.

The common thread running through all these northern cultures is an eagerness to be outdoors. Space age fabrics and insulation make dressing for the cold easier and less cumbersome than ever before. I would never discount the comfort of sitting beside a warm wood stove with a cup of hot chocolate on a blustery winter day, but I believe the key to celebrating winter is just getting outside.

Nagano on TV

It's been more than two months since the Nagano Winter Olympics, and I think I've calmed down enough to discuss the Games without losing my temper. But I'm still mad! I feel cheated. Most Americans tolerate the pathetic television coverage of the Winter Olympics for two reasons: first, except for the fortunate few who live close enough to Canada to watch CBC, we have no alternative; and second, most Americans haven't attended an Olympic Games in person, and therefore don't know what they're missing.

I may sound unjustly critical, but as a member of six previous Winter Olympic teams, I do know what we're all missing here at home. I've experienced that rush of adrenaline marching into the opening ceremony, and I've endured the crushing frustration of a sub-standard performance on the one day I wanted so badly to do my best.

With more than one hundred fifty distinct competitions at Nagano, in fourteen different sports, involving more than two thousand athletes, from seventy nations, there was an abundance of thrilling victories and agonizing defeats to satisfy even the most jaded sports fan. But CBS blew it, and it had nothing to do with delaying broadcasts for prime-time viewing audience back home.

To be fair, CBS deserves credit for some aspects of their coverage of the Winter Olympics. They demonstrated the technological capacity to televise entire race courses, from start to finish. In the men's downhill or the bobsled, for example, we saw far more of the competition than the spectators at the site in Japan, who braved blizzards and fog to catch a glimpse of one blur of colorful Lycra after another.

As an extra bonus, we saw the most exciting moments over and over, thanks to instant replay. Each time I watched Austria's Hermann Maier cartwheel through those snow fences, I was more astounded that he came back to win gold in the giant slalom and the super G.

And CBS had the resources to research and present interesting historical information. As a competitor in the Sapporo Olympics, I remember the euphoria that engulfed Japan when Yukio Kasaya led his teammates to a sweep in the normal hill ski jump. But I found it interesting to learn how heavily that victory weighed upon the shoulders of Japan's current ski jumpers. I also remember Janet Lynn's spunk and grace in accepting a bronze medal instead of gold, but I had no idea she was such a sweetheart of the Japanese people, still a celebrity there after twenty-six years.

But sadly, what CBS did right is overshadowed by what they did wrong. For starters, they promised us more than 120 hours of coverage. I suspect what they actually meant was 40 hours of commercials, 40 hours of studio gossip and celebrity interviews in the broadcast center, and perhaps 40 hours of actual event coverage. Of the fourteen different sports contested at Nagano, figure skating seemed to account for at least a third of the air time. I have nothing against figure skating. I especially admire the skill and strength of the pairs. But do the CBS producers honestly believe that most of us would prefer to watch Tara Lipinski and Michelle Kwan *practice*, rather than catch a glimpse of Norwegian phenomenon Bjorn Daehlie make Olympic history by winning an astounding eight gold medals in cross-country skiing?

CBS is not a novice at broadcasting sports. They have successfully covered major professional and college games for decades. What makes them think that at the Olympics, with so many exciting events every day, we long to see their co-hosts chit-chat endlessly in a studio?

And as if there wasn't enough drama at the Nagano Games, CBS had to fabricate more by bringing Tanya Harding and Nancy Kerrigan together for an interview. CBS created a circus sideshow out of the Tanya/Nancy incident in 1994, and they couldn't resist beating the same dead horse one more time in Nagano.

Sorry, but even after two months, I'm still angry, and you would be too, if you knew what you've been missing. If you really enjoy winter sports, make plans right now to be in Salt Lake City for the 2002 Winter Games. Seeing the Olympics in person is an entirely different show.

A Reunion in Alaska

One of the most colorful and widely recognized U.S. military units of World War II was the Tenth Mountain Division, the brainchild of Charles "Minnie" Dole. Originally assigned to Fort Lewis, Washington, near the year-round snowfields of Mount Ranier, Minnie's Ski Troops consisted mainly of volunteers who had experience in skiing or mountaineering. Following fierce combat in Northern Italy during the winter of 1945, which resulted in the Allied advance to Germany, the Tenth Mountain Division was sent home to Camp Hale, Colorado, and disbanded before the end of that year.

A decade later, the U.S. was preparing to host the 1960 Winter Olympics at Squaw Valley, California. Biathlon, a sport combining cross-country skiing and rifle marksmanship, would be returning to the Olympic program after a hiatus of thirty-six years. In the winter of 1957, the first biathlon competition in the U.S. was held, appropriately, at Camp Hale, the former home of the Tenth Mountain Division.

The army recognized both the military-skills aspect, and public relations value of a training center for biathlon competitors. After considering the renovation of Camp Hale in Colorado, ultimately Fort Richardson, on the outskirts of Anchorage, Alaska, was selected. For the following two decades, the biathletes who represented the U.S. at World Championships and Winter Olympic Games, all trained at Fort Richardson.

Like the veterans of the Tenth Mountain Division, many of whom used their skiing experience to establish winter resorts, manufacture improved ski equipment, or publish magazines devoted to the sport, many veterans of the Biathlon Training Center have also remained involved in skiing. The following is just a sample of former biathletes who returned to the Northeast after serving there.

Terry Aldrich of Cornwall, Vermont, became the dean of NCAA ski coaches, having directed the Middlebury College Ski Team for nearly thirty years. Don Cochrane put Mountain Top Nordic Center in Chittenden, Vermont, on the map by making snow for cross-country when Mother Nature wouldn't cooperate. Larry Damon helped hundreds of visitors to the Trapp Family Lodge in Stowe, Vermont, get more fun out of winter thanks to his excellent ski instruction.

Dennis Donahue coached high school skiers at Holderness School and through the Ford Sayre Ski Council in Hanover, New Hampshire, as well as his own three children, two of whom captained Dartmouth Ski Teams. Marty Hall coached the U.S. Nordic Team during the glory days of Bill Koch's Olympic silver medal, then moved north of the border to achieve similar success with Canadian cross-country skiers. Marty then moved back to the States to coach at Bowdoin College in Maine.

For many years, Ford Hubbard of East Burke, Vermont, helped build ski resorts across the country for sno-engineering, but recently he returned home to assume control of Burke Mountain. In spite of assignments all over the world for IBM, Charlie Kellogg found time to serve on the board of directors of the U.S. Biathlon Association and remain at the top of the results sheets in regional and national masters cross-country competitions. In the late 1960s, Phil Savignano was one of a handful of junior athletes invited to train at Fort Rich during the summer. Since then, Phil directed the Outdoor Discovery Program for L.L.Bean, and then became the outdoor programs coordinator at Pineland Farms in New Gloucester, Maine.

And Jed Williamson followed his Fort Richardson days with a varied career oriented toward the outdoors. His mountaineering credentials include expeditions on Denali and Everest as well as a term as the president of the American Alpine Club. He served as executive director of the U.S. Biathlon Association for several years before assuming the presidency of Sterling College in Craftsbury Common, Vermont.

In 2002, at the Salt Lake Winter Olympics, several survivors of "The Unit" at Fort Rich began to generate enthusiasm for a reunion. During the final week of July in 2004 more than sixty former biathlon competitors and their families gathered in Alaska to swap lies about training and racing thirty years ago. Anchorage was ready for us.

Celebrate Winter

Nordic Skiing Returns to Aroostook County, 2000

Aroostook County is the northernmost part of Maine. It's known primarily for vast stretches of evergreen forests, gently rolling potato fields, and severe winters. During the winter of 1999–2000, the town of Allagash made national headlines by recording a winter temperature of fifty-two degrees below zero, Fahrenheit. Aroostook County is so far north that during the height of the Cold War, the Air Force established a strategic air command base, featuring a runway two and a half miles long, near the town of Limestone. It was a quicker flight from Loring to Moscow than from any other base in the lower forty-eight states.

Skiing in the eastern U.S. had its origins in Aroostook County. Back in 1870, several dozen Swedish immigrants to the U.S. were lured to northern Maine by the promise of a better life, 100 acres of free land, and a dollar a day to clear fields and build roads. Skiing was not a sport in those days; it was a necessary means of transportation during the long cold winters. By the early 1900s Fredrick Jorgensen of New Sweden, Maine, had established a widespread reputation as a dedicated game warden who, thanks to his prowess on skis, struck fear into the hearts of many poachers.

The 1930s brought lavish winter carnivals to Aroostook County, week-long, mid-winter festivals that featured ski jumping and cross-country events. In spite of temperatures hovering at thirty below, the highlight of the 1937 Fort Fairfield Winter Carnival was the Tri-Town Ski Marathon, a 35-mile loop that linked Caribou to Presque Isle and Fort Fairfield, which was skied three days in a row.

Ironically, it was plowed roads, World War II and the Tenth Mountain Division that signaled an end to the glory days of Nordic skiing in northern Maine. With the widespread plowing of the county's roads in the 1930s, cross-country skiing was no longer a necessity of winter survival. And when the veterans of the famous Tenth Mountain Division returned from Europe after the war and began establishing Alpine ski resorts across the country, Nordic skiing all but disappeared in Aroostook County.

That is, until a fortuitous coincidence. Andy Shepard, who was responsible for winter sports equipment at L.L.Bean, accompanied his son to the Maine High School Ski Championships in Fort Kent. Andy was impressed by the energy and enthusiasm displayed by the parents who organized and hosted that event, and equally impressed by the deep blanket of snow that covered northern Aroostook County, even late in the winter, when southern Maine had been barren for weeks.

At the same time, Max Cobb, the national program director for the U.S. biathlon team, had been evaluating some interesting information he had learned from his Scandinavian counterparts. Even in Norway and Sweden, where Nordic skiing has been a matter of national pride for generations, fewer promising athletes were being drawn from the major cities into the challenging sports of cross-country and biathlon. It appeared that most of the recent Olympic hopefuls were from tiny villages in the most remote regions of Scandinavia.

Max and Andy put their discoveries together in the form of a proposal to the Libra Foundation, a charitable trust in Portland established by the late Betty Noyce "to benefit the people of Maine." Their timing couldn't have been better. The Defense Department had recently decommissioned Loring Air Force Base, depriving Aroostook County of thousands of jobs, and millions of dollars in revenue. In addition, Maine's popular governor, Angus King, was promoting the theme for his second term. The phrase "One Maine" was an acknowledgement that northern and interior Maine had not shared the recent economic boom enjoyed by the southern and coastal regions.

The Libra Foundation embraced Max and Andy's plan to reintroduce Nordic skiing to Aroostook County, and work began in the summer of 1999. Phase one of the project focused on grassroots development: making Nordic skiing as accessible to the youth of northern Maine as Little League Baseball is elsewhere in America. Trails were planned to be within walking distance of the schools in New Sweden, Stockholm, Fort Kent, Caribou, Presque Isle, Van Buren, and Fort Fairfield. At least as many additional trails were planned for development in other towns the following summer. Enthusiastic community volunteers pitched in and three of the newly designed trails were in use the first winter. A 50-kilometer ski marathon trail was planned, with the hope that it would link some of the county's skiing communities and provide an opportunity to reestablish the exciting distance skiing events of the 1930s.

Phase two of the project included the hiring of an international-caliber director, as well as world-class coaches for cross-country and biathlon. Max Saenger, a veteran of the Dartmouth College Ski Team and the Swiss World Cup Biathlon Team, was installed as the executive director of the Maine Winter Sports Center. Max conducted clinics and workshops for Aroostook County Nordic coaches and skiers, while also supervising the search for two world-class Nordic coaches. As the dedicated young skiers of northern Maine progressed through their school ski teams, experienced international coaches were available to guide them toward their goal of representing the U.S. at the Winter Olympic Games.

Phase three of the Maine Winter Sports Center focused on the creation of two world-class, Nordic skiing venues, one in Fort Kent, the other between Caribou and Presque Isle. These facilities were planned to be comparable to the finest Nordic racing centers in Europe, with challenging trails, comfortable lodges, convenient spectator areas, and even paved roller-skiing loops for summer training. These two sites were meant to draw major national and international Nordic competitions to Aroostook County, exposing the local skiers to the world's best athletes.

It was anticipated that eventually the excellent facilities, the world-class coaching, the reliable snow, and the local enthusiasm for Nordic skiing would draw talented Olympic hopefuls from other parts of the country to live, train and compete in Aroostook County. And so there were plans to establish a Nordic Ski Academy in facilities on the former Loring Air Force Base, in conjunction with local school districts and the state university system, which would allow students to pursue their Olympic dream without sacrificing their academic goals.

Every successful Olympic sport in the U.S. has found a community it can call home. For decades, our best distance runners lived and trained in

Eugene, Oregon. The dominance of American swimmers was synonymous with Mission Viejo, California, and the emergence of successful American cyclists was linked to Boulder, Colorado. American Nordic skiers may have finally found an ideal home in far northern Maine. It shouldn't have been a surprise that members of the U.S. cross-country and biathlon teams to the 2006 Olympics in Turin, Italy, listed their home as Aroostook County, Maine.

Finnish Skiers Open Pandora's Box

Finland, about the size of Montana, lies entirely above the 60th parallel and is blanketed in snow for much of the year. As a result, the Finns are passionate about winter sports.

It was the Finnish ice hockey team that stood between the U.S. and the gold medal at the Lake Placid Winter Olympics. Young, cocky Matti Nykaenen dominated ski jumping in the 1980s. And the history of cross-country skiing is written with names like Hakulinen, Maentyranta, Hamalainen, and Mieto: men who often persevered through raging blizzards or bone-numbing cold to achieve Olympic glory. Since the inclusion of the cross-country relay on the Winter Olympics program in 1936, no other nation has won more medals in that event than Finland.

It is this magnificent winter sports tradition that make the revelations of 2001 so intensely painful. Through the decades, scores of World Cup competitions have been held in Lahti, Finland, often before crowds of one hundred thousand devoted fans. In February 2001, for the sixth time since 1928, Lahti hosted the Nordic Skiing World Championships, an eleven-day gathering of the best Nordic competitors, representing nearly thirty nations from around the globe.

Soon after the races began, Finnish sports enthusiasts were shocked to learn that three-time Olympic medalist, Jari Isometsa had failed the doping control for the men's pursuit. Officials reported that Isometsa had used hydroxyethel starch, an intravenous plasma expander, commonly called HES. Within days, the recently established World Anti-Doping Agency demanded a surprise testing of the entire Finnish Nordic team.

In a tragic twist of fate, on the day Finland defeated their arch rival, Norway, in the men's relay, three members of that victorious Finnish team tested positive for using HES. Adding to the national disgrace, two top Finnish women also failed drug tests. Especially painful for Finland was the realization that the six cheaters included two of their national heroes. Mika Myllyla was the Olympic 30-kilometer champion in Nagano and won three gold medals at the 1999 World Championships. Harri Kirvesniemi was a national icon, having brought home to Finland a medal from each of the past six Winter Olympics!

With endurance events like cross-country skiing, a significant key to success is the amount of oxygen an athlete can transport from the lungs to the muscles. Competitors with a higher concentration of red blood cells transport more oxygen, and thus, can work harder, longer. Erythropoietin (EPO) is a natural substance produced by the kidneys to stimulate red blood cell production. Synthetic EPO is used by doctors to treat anemia, but it's also popular among unethical endurance athletes, to improve their performance.

Training at high altitude also stimulates red cell production. The Finns took this concept a step further by constructing a pressurized team house, where their skiers slept at the atmospheric equivalent of a 15,000-foot mountain top. But to adjust their athletes' hematocrits to concentrations permitted by the International Ski Federation, the Finnish team doctors had to administer the plasma expander, HES, which, in turn, was identified by the doping control.

No doubt, the glorious Finnish skiing tradition has been irreparably damaged, but clearly, the Finns were not the only ones who have been cheating. Unfortunately, the extent of scandal at the Lahti World Championships appears to be just one more example of athletes, coaches and team physicians who will do anything to win.

Dartmouth Skiers Win the NCAA Championship

Since 1954, the National Collegiate Athletic Association has hosted an annual championship of the top college and university skiers in the nation. The competition has undergone significant revisions through the years. Originally the championship drew only men who competed in downhill, slalom, cross-country and jumping. A restriction on team size insured that several members were versatile enough to ski multiple events, and the coveted Skimeister award went to the top four-event skier.

In the mid 1970s, following a couple of tragic accidents, the downhill was replaced by a giant slalom. Less than a decade later, the half dozen coaches who formed the NCAA Skiing Committee decided to drop jumping from the championship in favor of a second cross-country event, and in the process sounded the death knell for high school ski jumping programs from Maine to Alaska. In 1983, the NCAA expanded the championship to include women's skiing, creating an innovative, co-educational format, one of the first in collegiate sports.

In the early days of NCAA skiing, as the story goes, Willy Schaeffler, the legendary coach of Denver University, warned his colleagues from other schools of the potential inequity that could be created by recruiting European racers who were older, more experienced and nurtured in a culture that celebrated skiing excellence. When his rival coaches discounted his concerns, Willy was said to remark, "Well then, I'll show them how it's done." Before moving on to coach the U.S. Alpine Ski Team, Willy Schaeffler had won 11 NCAA titles for Denver with the help of a steady stream of European recruits.

This was a problem for several reasons. To begin with, the schools that traditionally competed in skiing included large universities as well as small, private colleges. While the universities representing states with a vibrant ski industry, like Colorado, Utah and Vermont, were able to offer attractive skiing scholarships to potential applicants, the smaller schools, like Middlebury, Williams and Dartmouth, could offer only need-based financial aid rather than athletic scholarships. To compound the problem, top American skiers attending the smaller schools would occasionally be lured off campus by the U.S. Ski Team, certainly a tribute to the college's ski program, but creating a painful void on the school's NCAA roster. Meanwhile, the foreign athletes skiing for the big universities were obligated by their scholarship agreements to compete in the NCAAs. That first combined championship in 1983 was won by a powerful team from the University of Utah, comprised of four Alpine men, four Alpine women, four Nordic men, and four Nordic women. Sixteen ski racers on the NCAA Championship team, and only four of them were Americans.

An especially enjoyable aspect of the NCAA Skiing Championship, from the perspective of the athletes and coaches, is the event's migration across the nation's snowbelt from year to year. Although there is excitement about skiing in Montana, Colorado, and Alaska, there are also additional challenges. Western snow is typically bountiful, but for Alpine racers that can translate into ruts rather than the boilerplate they're accustomed to in the East. For the Nordic skiers, the issue is altitude. While Anchorage is at sea level, courses in Utah, New Mexico and Colorado can be in air thin enough to make the Eastern skiers see spots. I raced for Middlebury College years ago, and experienced firsthand the Nordic "sucking chest wound" at the 1968 NCAAs in Steamboat Springs, Colorado.

I should confess before I continue that I coached the Dartmouth men's team from 1978 through 1989, and although we had an impressive array of individual NCAA champions, and sent more than a few skiers on to U.S. Olympic teams, we were never a legitimate contender for the NCAA team title. All of which makes Dartmouth's 2007 NCAA Championship so impressive to me. Closer examination of the results reveals that it was truly a team victory, solid skiing by all the participants rather than spectacular performances by a few. It certainly helped that the event was in the East, so that altitude was not a factor for the Nordic skiers. And, no doubt, the team's third-place finish in last winter's NCAAs, in addition to an unbeaten record in the 2007 winter carnival competitions, gave the Big

Green the confidence that victory at the NCAAs was finally within their grasp.

Dartmouth's 2007 national title in skiing should be an inspiration to young student athletes across the country. Congratulations to the skiers and coaches at Dartmouth who demonstrated that hard work, both in the classroom and on the ski slopes can lead to victory.

Celebrate Winter

The World Returns to Aroostook County, 2010

In 1999, Maine's governor, Angus King, commissioned an economic study that determined that New England's largest state was actually two distinct economic regions: the affluent southeastern coast and the struggling northern forests. Through the years, Aroostook County had been dealt a hat trick of economic setbacks: first, the emergence of Idaho as the nation's premier source of potatoes; second, Quebec's ability to process timber products more economically than Maine; and more recently, the Defense Department's decision to close Loring Air Force Base in Limestone, eliminating thousands of civilian jobs.

What Aroostook County continued to have in abundance, however, was long, cold winters, reliable natural snow, and residents who valued hard work. Andy Shepard, formerly a winter sports manager for L.L.Bean, and Max Cobb, the driving force behind the U.S. biathlon team, recognized the potential of northern Maine and approached the Libra Foundation of Portland with a plan to "reestablish Nordic skiing as a lifestyle to stimulate the local economy and inspire the youth of northern Maine."

Eleven years later, during the first two weeks of February, Presque Isle and Fort Kent hosted the International Biathlon Union's World Cups #7 and #8, welcoming athletes, coaches, journalists and fans from thirty nations to "The Crown of Maine." Presque Isle, with a population of just under ten thousand, and Fort Kent with two thousand residents, braced for as many as thirty-five thousand spectators during the ten days of biathlon competitions and related festivities. The sport had become hugely popular throughout Europe and the events in northern Maine were televised live to an estimated 120 million viewers across the Atlantic. For several days in early February, devoted biathlon fans from northern Norway to the heel of the Italian boot were glued to their televisions as their favorite athletes ski and shoot in the wilds of northern Maine.

Adding to the excitement for American spectators was the participation of a promising U.S. team. Tim Burke of Paul Smiths, New York, led the World Cup standings prior to the Olympic break, the first time any U.S. biathlete had achieved that distinction. Both Lowell Bailey of Lake Placid and Laura Spector of Lenox, Massachusetts, had earned top-thirty finishes in prior World Cup events. Other U.S. team members who had lived and trained in northern Maine enjoyed a "home court advantage."

Creating competition facilities in northern Maine capable of hosting world-caliber events was a team effort requiring a diverse set of skills. A Nordic race venue in Fort Kent made sense because there was a well-established community ski club, desirable terrain not far from town, and a cadre of volunteers with experience hosting major winter events. Although the base lodge of the Lone Pine Alpine ski hill was a logical focal point for all ski club activities, the only suitable location for a biathlon shooting range was in a natural bowl beyond the top of the ski lift, thus requiring a new start/finish area, warming lodge, and racing trail network at the top of the hill. With funding from the Libra Foundation, the community of Fort Kent pitched in and within months was ready to host biathlon events. Their first Biathlon World Cup event in 2004 received rave reviews from international athletes, IBU officials and the hundreds of spectators who attended.

A different challenge faced what would become the Nordic Heritage Center on the Presque Isle/Fort Fairfield town line. Much of northern Aroostook County consists of gently rolling potato fields. A successful competition venue must be relatively close to the population concentration; in northern Maine that means Presque Isle and Caribou. Only one significant, undeveloped ridge in the area fit the requirements, but it was carved into nearly a dozen private parcels. The Nordic Heritage Center would never have been possible without the determination and negotiating skill of Brian Hamel, a Presque Isle community activist who saw the potential of the project and secured the rights to all the necessary land.

A decade prior, Andy Shepard, Max Cobb and others envisioned the reestablishment of Nordic skiing in northern Maine as a boost to the regional economy and an inspiration to the local youth. During the ten days of the IBU World Cup biathlon events in early February 2010, an estimated $15 million circulated through the communities of Aroostook County. In addition, several American athletes who made their home in the county, including a few who were born there, represented the Maine Winter Sports Center and the U.S. in competitions across the country and throughout the world. In just over a decade, Max and Andy's vision for reestablishing skiing in northern Maine became a reality.

Celebrate Winter

Let the Women Jump

I love the Olympic Games. Of course, I'm far from objective since I've been involved in seven Winter Olympics in various capacities. But I'm enough of a romantic idealist to still believe in Baron Pierre de Coubertin's vision of bringing together the youth of the world in an international celebration of inspiring athletic competition. In the words of Bud Greenspan, who made a career, spanning several decades, filming unforgettable Olympic moments, "Ask not alone for victory, ask for courage. For if you can endure you bring honour to yourself. Even more, you bring honour to us all."

I am not such a big fan of the International Olympic Committee, the organization responsible for keeping de Coubertin's vision alive. Members of the IOC tend to take themselves too seriously, in my opinion, often expecting, even demanding VIP treatment everywhere they go. Some of the dark underbelly of the IOC's methods was revealed in the bribery scandal preceding the 2002 Salt Lake City Winter Games. I also believe that the IOC has, until very recently, ignored the growing cancer of illegal performance enhancement, or doping in Olympic sports, out of a fear of tarnishing the image and therefore the marketing value of the five rings.

I'll be the first to acknowledge that the IOC has faced some very thorny issues. When de Coubertin revived the Olympic Games in 1896, he envisioned a gathering of amateur sportsmen (and women) who participated purely for the joy of competition. Professional athletes were virtually unknown at the time. But by the final decades of the twentieth century, athletes who made a living at their sport were commonplace, and a strict interpretation of the amateurism rules would have eliminated many of the world's best from Olympic competition.

Inevitably, the IOC becomes embroiled in politics. Because the whole world is watching, the Olympics become a vehicle for every cause to get their message to a global audience. The most tragic example was the attack of Palestinian terrorists during the 1972 Munich Summer Games, which resulted in the death of eleven Israeli athletes. In 1976, several African nations boycotted the Montreal Olympics to protest New Zealand's rugby team playing a match in apartheid South Africa. Four years later, the Moscow Games were marred by the absence of large delegations from the U.S., Japan and West Germany, all protesting the Soviet Union's invasion of Afghanistan. Four years later, much of the Communist bloc reciprocated by keeping their athletes home from Los Angles. Appearing relatively mild by comparison, were last summer's demonstrations, drawing attention to China's human rights violations and appeals for Tibet's freedom, during the Olympic torch run.

Having thus acknowledged the difficult decisions the IOC has faced through the decades, I can't understand their position on the current controversy, their refusal to permit ski jumping events for women at next winter's Olympics in Vancouver. According to recent news reports, it seems to me that IOC President Jocques Rogge is hiding behind a flimsy technicality, requiring a sport to have had at least two World Championship events before it can be considered for inclusion on the Olympic program.

Not long ago, ski jumping rivaled biathlon, ice hockey and bobsled as the most macho of all winter Olympic sports. For generations, ski jumping was the domain of tough, steel-nerved, dare devils who were willing to squat on massive skis thundering down an icy in-run at 70 miles per hour, then launch themselves into the air. In addition to raw courage, the sport required powerful thighs and excellent timing. Then, a young, innovative jumper discovered that by spreading his skis from the traditional parallel position into a V in flight, he achieved greater lift, and thus a longer jump. Soon, the medal winners in major jumping competitions no longer looked like NFL halfbacks with thighs like tree trunks, but like young boys who floated to bottom of the hill. And the girls were not far behind.

As with most issues in international sports, I'm sure politics plays a role. I suspect the Canadian and American women have been quick to gain experience and expertise in ski jumping, while their typically conservative, European counterparts have been slower to adopt the sport.

As a result, those European nations, historically strong in jumping, will be reluctant to support an expansion to include women's events. I also suspect there is a little concern among the "good ol' boys" that one of these scrappy, determined, 100-pound women will be the one setting the distance records on all the ski jumping hills.

Better get used to it, guys. Just let the women jump!

Celebrate Winter

A Skier's Guide to the Vancouver Winter Olympics

In the past, the skiing at the Winter Olympic Games was straightforward. The glamorous events were the Alpine disciplines (which originated in the European Alps): slalom, giant slalom and downhill. Slalom required technical proficiency, while downhill demanded raw courage. Nordic skiing (from the Nordic countries of Scandinavia) was divided into four disciplines: cross-country, biathlon, jumping and Nordic combined. Cross-country consisted of four events for men: a 15 kilometer, a 30 kilometer, a 4x10-kilometer relay, and the signature endurance event, the 50 kilometer. Shorter events were added to the Olympic program for women in 1964.

Biathlon, a combination of cross-country skiing and rifle marksmanship, consisted of a distance (20 kilometers) and a relay event (4x10 kilometers) until 1980 when a 10-kilometer sprint was added. Women's biathlon became a part of the Olympics in Albertville in 1992. Jumping was comprised of two competitions, the 70-meter hill and the 90-meter hill. Those designations represented how far a good jumper might safely fly, on a good ride. Nordic combined married the two incongruous talents of jumping and cross-country with an innovative and exciting pursuit format. The results of the 70-meter jumping event are mathematically converted to time. The winner of the jump leads off the 15-kilometer cross-country with his rivals chasing from appropriate intervals behind. The first across the finish line is the Nordic combined champion.

In 1956 at Cortina, Italy, television got into the act. Before long, events that were easily covered by TV — ice hockey, figure skating and ski jumping, for example — gained additional exposure, and thus, popularity. Less telegenic sports — like cross-country skiing — languished in obscurity. Soon, the winter sport governing bodies revised their events to make them more accessible to TV and even proposed new events, custom made for it.

Ironically, ski jumping, made famous decades ago by ABC's *Wide World of Sports* "agony of defeat" image, seems to have lost popularity relative to the other skiing sports. The two events have been renamed the normal hill and the large hill competitions, and a team competition has been added. Jumping missed a golden opportunity to double its exposure by adding women's events, but I suspect some of the traditional "ol' boys" were afraid the fearless, young women would outdistance the heavier men.

In former times, the skier who had the best results in the slalom, giant slalom and downhill was crowned the Alpine combined champion. In Vancouver, super combined events in downhill and slalom will recognize the most versatile skiers. In 1988, in Calgary, a super giant slalom was added to the Alpine format, not quite as hell-bent as the downhill, but less technical than the giant slalom.

Nordic combined has expanded its program from the original, normal hill jump followed by a pursuit cross-country ski race. In addition to that event, the Nordic combined athletes also have a team competition that includes jumping and a 4x5 kilometer relay. Finally, the Nordic combined skiers move to the large hill followed by a 10-kilometer cross-country race.

Thanks to its popularity on European television, biathlon has prospered at the Olympics. From one event at the 1960 Squaw Valley Games, the current biathlon schedule includes ten events, five for men and five for women. All shooting is now at metal, knock-down targets so that hits are instantaneously visible to the spectators, and the majority of events are either pursuit or mass start, to maximize viewer excitement.

In the early 1980s the skating technique transformed cross-country skiing so that the current schedule is a creative mixture of traditional, kick and glide, or classic technique, and the newer skating, or free technique. Of the twelve events on the cross-country program all but two are now head-to-head pursuit format or mass start to stimulate spectator excitement. Four competitions will require both techniques within the event.

Originally known as "hot doggers," freestyle skiers debuted at the '92 Albertville Olympics. Since then their thigh-burning mogul runs and unbelievable aerial contortions have become a favorite of television audiences around the world. Head-to-head ski cross events for men and women will add even more thrills to the freestyle program in Vancouver.

It's hard to imagine that a few years ago, snowboarding was forbidden at many Alpine ski areas. Since then the sport has exploded, reenergizing the entire snow sport industry. At this Olympics, boarders will compete in three spectator-pleasing events: the half pipe, a parallel giant slalom and the snowboard cross (as much NASCAR as ski racing).

The great news for all of us skiing fanatics is that there will be far more to see at the Vancouver Games. The bad news: we'll still have to endure hours of commercials and mind-numbing chatter by studio hosts to ferret out the action on the slopes.

Celebrate Winter

U.S. Nordic Skiing Loses a Couple of Champions

When I discovered cross-country ski racing in the mid 1960s, the sport was just beginning to emerge from obscurity. Putney, Vermont, Hanover, New Hampshire, and Rumford, Maine, all boasted knowledgeable coaches, challenging race courses and promising young athletes. For the first time, young women, inspired by Putney's Martha Rockwell, were encouraged to try the sport. And for at least a decade of those formative years, the athlete that all young American cross-country skiers emulated was Mike Gallagher.

Gallagher, who grew up in Rutland, Vermont, owed his remarkable athletic success to four essential components: first, he inherited a great motor from his parents, which translated into world-class endurance; second, due in part to John Caldwell's coaching and a feisty rivalry with Bob Gray and Mike Elliott, Gallagher developed excellent skiing technique; third, also thanks to Gray and Elliott, Gallagher thrived on training hard; and finally, Gallagher simply celebrated the time he was training and racing — there was nothing he would rather be doing.

I remember a U.S. team training hike (actually, a day-long trail run) on the Appalachian Trail from the Mahoosucs in Maine to the AMC hut at Pinkham Notch, New Hampshire. Although the workout had clearly been designated as "long, slow distance," within a few miles it became a no-holds-barred race, with most of us trying desperately not to be dropped by Gallagher and Gray.

Stopping for a quick drink of water and visit to the outhouse at a trailside campsite, Gallagher discovered an abandoned cast iron skillet. While Bob Gray was using the facilities, Gallagher slipped the heavy skillet into Gray's daypack and swore the rest of us to silence. The brief break over, Gallagher hustled us back on the trail and the race resumed. Mike's prank backfired when Gray appeared not to notice the extra weight, and had no trouble keeping up. At lunch, Bob seemed pleased to discover the large, cast iron skillet, and carried it the remainder of the workout. This intensified Gallagher's competitive drive so that the rest of us had no chance of keeping up through the afternoon.

That fierce spirit earned Mike nine U.S. National Championships, trips to three FIS World Championships, and a spot on three U.S. Winter Olympics teams. He has been inducted into several athletic and skiing halls of fame. While many elite athletes struggle after retiring from competition, Mike maintained his connection to the sport as a successful and respected coach, including seventeen years at the high school level and six years for the U.S. Ski Team.

Mike Gallagher died unexpectedly on his seventy-second birthday, October 3, 2013. A gathering to celebrate his life, held at his home in the heart of the Green Mountains, drew friends, family members and several generations of America's Nordic skiing community to recognize Mike's lifelong contributions to the sport.

On the other side of the country, Peter Hale, age sixty-six, lost a long struggle with cancer on November seventeenth, at his home in Bozeman, Montana. Peter was introduced to Nordic skiing in 1970 at the U.S. Army's Biathlon Training Center in Alaska, and the relationship intensified for more than forty years. Growing up in Minneapolis, Peter excelled at cross-country running and ice hockey, which allowed him to pick up Nordic skiing relatively quickly. Throughout the 1970s, Peter competed in cross-country skiing and biathlon events, including several National Championships and Olympic Tryouts.

When he retired from competition, he was immediately in demand as a manufacturer's representative for several lines of Nordic skiing products, and quickly became the champion of the struggling, young athlete. Dozens, perhaps scores of young skiers and biathletes progressed and eventually broke through to achieve international recognition because Peter Hale recognized their talent.

At the 1992 Winter Olympics in Albertville, Peter was helping in the U.S. biathlon team wax room. The morning of the 50-kilometer cross-country event was a waxing nightmare, new fallen snow at the freezing point. The Soviet Union had unraveled months earlier, and just prior to the Opening Ceremony, the International Olympic Committee had decided to allow the three Baltic countries to compete as independent nations. As the men's 50 kilometer got underway, a frantic Latvian coach appealed for help: "Vee haf no vax for dis snow." Peter exchanged a quick glance with the other American coaches, then took the Latvian's skis into the wax cabin. Moments later, a tearful Latvian coach was running to the start with Peter Hale's best effort on his athlete's skis. Hours later, we learned that the sole Latvian, representing his new nation for the first time, in his first Olympic Games, had had the race of his life.

That is Peter Hale's legacy, with a wry smile and a quick joke, giving the underdog a chance to compete with the best.

Celebrate Winter

The Russian Riddle

In an October 1939 radio address, Winston Churchill described Russia as "a riddle, wrapped in a mystery, inside an enigma." I know what he was talking about. In 1974 I competed in the Biathlon World Championships, hosted in Minsk, at the time part of the Soviet Union. We saw imposing buildings and impressive statues along expansive boulevards that were almost totally devoid of vehicles, except for military trucks belching clouds of diesel exhaust. We saw grim-faced residents, bundled against the cold, patiently waiting outside grocery shops, the shelves inside virtually bare. I was fearfully approached by a Russian woman who in broken English asked if I would sell her ski wax so that her husband could teach his physical education classes. And yet, more than 120,000 passionate spectators lined the biathlon course cheering the Soviet team on to victory in the men's relay event.

In 1989, I returned to the Soviet Union as part of a pioneering Outward Bound project joining a group of Vietnam veterans with younger Soviet vets from their conflict in Afghanistan. We were surprised to learn that the Soviet involvement in Afghanistan was largely kept secret from the population back in Russia, and that one of the largest militaries on the planet had virtually no organization comparable to our Veterans Health Administration, to assist the thousands of wounded combat vets, following their tours of duty.

During short home stays with our Soviet counterparts in the city of Tashkent, following the Outward Bound expedition, we experienced genuine friendship and warm hospitality from young soldiers who had been trained to regard us as mortal enemies. We also observed the crumbling infrastructure of the Soviet Union: city streets marred by bone-jarring potholes; bleak, dirty apartment buildings with inoperable elevators; inadequate sanitary facilities.

So when the 2014 Sochi Olympics approached, I was ambivalent. To be honest, Russia was not on the top of my "bucket list" for return visits. Adding to my quandary was a long-time friendship with Alexander

Tikhonov, one of the Soviet Union's most decorated athletes. Tikhonov and I had become friends at the 1969 Biathlon World Championships in Zakopane, Poland, a friendship that grew through his retirement from international competition at the 1980 Lake Placid Olympics.

After the breakup of the Soviet Union, Tikhonov's stature as a national sports hero and his competitive drive led him to wealth and notoriety as one of Russia's new oligarchs. But in 2007, my friend was implicated in a plot to murder a Siberian government official. Although sentenced to three years in prison, Tikhonov was immediately released thanks to an amnesty law. Under Tikhonov's leadership the Russian biathlon team was plagued by doping violations, and when he ran for the presidency of the International Biathlon Union, the U.S. delegation strongly opposed his candidacy. I was pretty certain Tikhonov would be a featured celebrity at Sochi, and I was nervous about reconnecting with him.

But the U.S. biathletes headed to Sochi comprised the strongest team we ever had. Tim Burke of Paul Smiths, New York, won a silver medal at the 2013 World Championship, while relative newcomer, Susan Dunklee of Barton, Vermont, had an impressive fifth-place finish. Anyone following the U.S. biathlon team knew that an Olympic medal was on the horizon, and winning it on Russian soil would be especially sweet. My wife, Kay, was understandably concerned about the security issues, but I reminded her that security has been a part of the Olympics for decades and one of the most unfortunate recent incidents occurred in Atlanta.

With some trepidation, we struggled through the Russian visa applications, made airline reservations, and wondered whether to pack for seaside palm trees or snow in the mountains. We shouldn't have worried. Even with the acknowledged graft and corruption, it's possible to build remarkable facilities with $51 billion. In a sparkling new, Bolshoy Ice Dome, we saw the U.S. men's hockey team defeat Russia in a nail-biting shootout. Long after dark, under brilliant flood lights, we watched the world's best ski jumpers soar the length of a football field and a half.

And high in the peaks above the new Alpine ski resort of Krasnaya Polyana, on a brutally challenging course, we watched our U.S. biathletes put together their best Olympic performance ever. Led by Lowell Bailey's impressive eighth place in the individual 20-kilometer event and Susan Dunklee's eleventh in the Women's 12.5-kilometer mass start, four Americans combined for nine top-twenty-five finishes in individual competitions, while both the mixed relay and the women's relay teams finished in the top half of the field. U.S. biathletes continue to improve in Olympic and world competitions. It is only a matter of time before we see a U.S. biathlete on the podium at the Winter Olympic Games.

Celebrate Winter

Reflections of an Old-Timer at the PyeongChang Winter Olympics

I've had the remarkable good fortune of attending ten Winter Olympic Games. I was a member of the U.S. biathlon team in 1972 at Sapporo and again in 1976 at Innsbruck. I was an assistant coach for the U.S. biathletes at the 1980 Games in Lake Placid. I served as team leader for the U.S. biathletes at Calgary in 1988, Albertville in 1992 and Lillehammer in 1994. Then, in 2002, I was the chief of course for the biathlon events during the Salt Lake City Olympics, a volunteer position that was every bit as stressful as competing back in 1972 and 1976.

At the most recent three Winter Games—Vancouver, Sochi and PyeongChang—my wife and I have enjoyed the relative luxury of attending as spectators, cheering on U.S. cross-country skiers and biathletes. As the jet lag from our trip home from South Korea began to wear off, I couldn't help thinking about the dramatic changes these two sports have experienced over the years. It seems to me that many of these changes can be traced to three factors: innovations by the athletes, technological improvements and the influence of television.

Back in 1972 we were on wooden skis, kick-waxed the entire length. There were two biathlon events, the 20 kilometer individual and the 4x7.5-kilometer relay. We shot large-caliber rifles on a 150-meter range using paper targets for the 20 kilometer and glass disks for the relay. It was impossible to determine the winner of the 20 kilometer until all the paper targets had been carefully inspected, sometimes hours after the conclusion of the event. A typical biathlon course consisted of three independent 4-kilometer loops, with cutoffs for the relay. Women didn't compete in biathlon at the Olympics until Albertville in 1992.

Men's cross-country skiing has been part of the Winter Olympics since the beginning in 1924 at Chamonix, France, when there was a 15-kilometer event as well as the legendary 50 kilometer. The first cross-country event for women was a 10 kilometer, which debuted in 1952. In those days, Nordic race courses consisted of roughly one-third climbing, one-third descent, and one-third relatively flat terrain. Well into the 1960s, courses were prepared by soldiers boot-packing or snowshoeing the course, followed by skiers stomping in the parallel tracks through the forests and fields. Competitors typically started at one-minute intervals, disappeared into the woods, only to reappear exhausted, often hours later, covered with frost and mucus. The men's 50-kilometer cross-country event at the 1932 Winter Olympics in Lake Placid consisted of a 25-kilometer loop skied twice, and was won by Finland's Veli Saarinen in four hours, twenty-eight minutes.

In my view, the first significant change came at the 1974 Nordic World Championships when Sweden's Thomas Magnusson won the men's 30 kilometer on Knessel synthetic skis. Fiberglass and metal had replaced wooden Alpine skis years earlier, but the faster plastic bases wouldn't hold Nordic kick wax. But in wet, heavy, painfully slow snow, Magnusson took a chance on the fiberglass Austrian skis and dominated the race. The headline in the Oslo paper the next day read something like: "Magnusson wins gold, Norwegian ski industry in peril."

The next major breakthrough occurred at the Innsbruck Olympics, two years later. Marty Hall, head coach of the U.S. cross-country team recruited Rob Kessel from Alpine skiing as his assistant. Together they determined that it was possible to wax the tips and tails of the new fiberglass skis for speed with Alpine wax, restricting the much slower cross-country kick wax to a short segment under the athlete's foot. This made the skis of the Americans faster than those of their European rivals and certainly contributed to Bill Koch's memorable silver medal in the 30 kilometer, the first and only Olympic medal in Nordic skiing for the U.S. until Kikkan Randall and Jessie Diggins struck gold in PyeongChang.

Following the success of the Innsbruck Olympics, expectations were high for U.S. Nordic skiers at the 1980 Olympics in Lake Placid. With a theoretical "home court advantage," Bill Koch's thirteenth in the men's 50 kilometer and Lyle Nelson's nineteenth in the biathlon 10-kilometer sprint fell short of the results that the public had been led to expect.

Discouraged, Koch elected to ski the international ski marathon circuit the following year rather than the Nordic World Cup. There, on trails groomed wide by Alpine-area Sno-Cats for thousands of citizen racers, he observed elite competitors pulling away from the throng by putting one ski in the set track and pushing off, skating-style, with the other. He quickly mastered this marathon-skate technique and began to experiment by skating with both skis. When he returned to the World Cup circuit a year later, he threw the Nordic world into turmoil by abandoning the relatively slow kick wax altogether and skating entire courses on skis waxed purely for speed. The result of Koch's persistence and innovation was a cumulative World Cup victory for the season, the first for the U.S. in cross-country skiing.

When the dust (or more accurately, snow) finally settled, Nordic skiing had two disciplines: classic (the traditional kicking and gliding) and freestyle (skating). Because biathlon was already complicated enough with skiing and shooting, they decided to go with skating as their designated technique, as did Nordic combined. In a type of mutual reinforcement cycle, the use of large Sno-Cat-type grooming machines on cross-country trails, which originally made the evolution of the skating technique possible, became a requirement once skating was accepted as a part of the sport.

Enter television. The first Winter Olympics to be televised were the 1956 Games, in Cortina, Italy, and it quickly became apparent how powerful the new medium could be. Figure skating, ice hockey and ski jumping immediately gained popularity, largely because they were relatively easy to cover. Alpine skiing, bobsled and Nordic skiing lagged behind because they were more difficult and expensive to film. The sports favored by TV prospered, enjoying increased funding from sponsors and a wave of young Olympic hopefuls. Meanwhile, those sports that were less telegenic scrambled to make their events more appealing to the camera. Nordic skiing and biathlon added mass-start and pursuit-format events, making it easy for spectators to see who was winning. In terms of spectator interest, biathlon had the advantage of the shooting range. With the adoption of the modern, knock-down targets and television's ability to in-set an athlete's target on the TV screen as the shot is taken, the popularity of the sport took off. In recent years, biathlon has become the most-watched winter sport in Europe with World Cup events rivaling the popularity of Monday Night Football in America.

In cross-country, one of the unintended consequences of the skating revolution was a focus on upper body strength, which in turn led some athletes to abandon kick wax in classic events and double-pole the entire course, especially in the shorter, sprint races. This led the FIS (the International Ski Federation) to require tougher courses with more challenging climbs.

As a result, what we saw in PyeongChang for both cross-country and biathlon were trails 30 feet wide, capable of accommodating three skaters side by side (without obstructing each other), with steeper climbs and faster, more challenging descents. Aside from the spacious start/finish stadiums, the traditional third of relatively flat terrain has disappeared. In PyeongChang there was also an effort to loop the trails back within sight of the spectators so that they saw more than just the start and finish of the events. For example, the men's 50 kilometer, perhaps the most iconic of the cross-country events, was conducted on two, 4.16-kilometer loops, which brought the competitors through the stadium in front of the cheering crowd a dozen times. The men's 50-kilometer classic in PyeongChang was won by Finland's Iivo Niskanen in a time of two hours, eight minutes (less than half the time it took for his countryman to complete the same distance in 1932 at Lake Placid).

Perhaps the most dramatic change was the scheduling of many of the Nordic skiing events at night (which allowed them to be televised live in Europe and the eastern U.S. at a reasonable hour). In addition to the expense of lighting and minimizing the number of TV camera platforms, another motivation for shorter ski loops is the growing need, thanks to climate change, to cover the entire trail with machine-made snow. Early in the winter the biathlon and cross-country courses were blanketed with a deep layer of machine-made snow, enough to survive warm temperatures and thaws well beyond the Olympic schedule in February.

While there have been advancements and technological improvements in other Winter Olympic sports, I can think of none more dramatic than what we've experienced in Nordic skiing. From a single biathlon event held at the 1960 Squaw Valley Games, there were ten biathlon competitions on the schedule at PyeongChang. With the advent of the skating technique, fiberglass skis, and fluorocarbon waxes, times for cross-country events have been cut in half in less than a generation. Thanks to machine-made snow, the 2022 Winter Olympic Games are scheduled to be hosted by Beijing, China, a city previously not known for winter sports. And through the development of LED lighting and high-definition television, the excitement of Nordic skiing events can be broadcast live, in prime time, to homes around the world.

Celebrate Winter

COACHING

The Joys of Roller Skiing

After eleven years as head coach of men's skiing at Dartmouth College, there are only a couple of incidents that I'd rather forget. Ironically, the most vivid doesn't even involve snow. Roller skiing is the most specific form of off-season training for cross-country. Equipped with ski poles and stubby, wheeled slats, similar to in-line skates, Nordic racers kick and glide or skate the back roads of New England throughout the summer and fall.

One of the many traditions I inherited when I began coaching at Dartmouth was a 50-kilometer roller ski time trial the Sunday before Thanksgiving. The event started on the Norwich town green and climbed through the hills to Union Village, on to Thetford, and finally back to Norwich. It was a grueling, three-hour endurance test, including several steep descents, two with sharp turns into classic covered bridges.

I had severe misgivings about the safety of the route, especially for the younger athletes who lacked experience on roller skis. But the time trial was a well-established tradition of the ski team, a rite of passage for the freshmen, and I hesitated to question any sacred Dartmouth traditions in my rookie year as coach.

After starting the athletes at one-minute intervals, I drove the van along the route, providing water stations and encouragement. By the time I reached the common on Thetford Hill, there was a thirty-minute spread between the faster and slower skiers.

When I approached the steep curve above the Union Village covered bridge, I thought I had overtaken everyone, but I couldn't be sure. As I climbed out of the van, my heart stopped. There was a ghastly smear of congealed blood across the road! I stared at the slippery red stain in horror, visualizing one of my skiers plowing into the hood of an oncoming car, the panicked driver throwing the broken body into the vehicle for a frantic rush to the hospital.

At that instant, one of my athletes thundered around the corner. He was crouched low, his legs spread, and his skis vibrating wildly on the rough pavement. Sparks flew from his pole tips as he dragged them in a futile effort to slow down. His eyes widened in terror as he approached the steep, twisting descent to the quaint covered bridge.

I sprinted full speed behind the skier and grabbed the waistband of his pants. As I slowed to a jog and then a walk, the color returned to his face. From a standing start, a hundred yards above the bridge, the turn was negotiable. I released my grip and watched the athlete roll smoothly into the opening of the bridge. Then, sickened by the smear of blood on the road, I sprinted back up the hill to intercept the next skier. One by one, the athletes roared into sight. I raced to catch them, slowed them to a stop, then bolted back up the hill.

Joe Cook, a local character whose house guards the entrance to the bridge, found this so entertaining that he pulled a lawn chair to the edge of his porch and sat down to enjoy the show. As I sprinted up and down the hill, Joe watched with the detached amusement of a world-class figure skating judge. When I was pretty sure all my skiers had passed the bloody corner, I hopped in the van and pulled onto the pavement. But in the rearview mirror I caught a glimpse of David Wilhauer, a freshman who had never roller skied before arriving at Dartmouth earlier that fall. He was hunched down in a bowlegged crouch and so petrified that he made not the slightest effort to reduce his speed. I slammed the van into PARK as David shot past. I scrambled from the seat, lunged and grabbed in one desperate motion! I felt the elastic waistband and yanked him to a stop like the arresting cable on an aircraft carrier. He was shaking uncontrollably and couldn't talk. Trying to sound calm, I said, "Take your skis and poles off. I'll go get the van. You've had enough training for today."

As I hiked the hill for the last time, Joe Cook stood and began to applaud. "Sunafagun, that was great! You fellas gonna do this ev'ry Sundee mornin'?"

"No way," I answered. "This is the last time as long as I'm the coach." As a dreaded afterthought, I asked, "Was there an accident here earlier?"

"What?" Joe seemed bewildered.

"All that blood on the road, did one of my guys get hit?"

Joe's face resolved into a broad smile. "Oh thet, Hell no! One 'a the Barker boys got hisself a nice little buck 'bout sunrise; had to drag it up the bank an' crost the road ta 'is pickup. Thet's deer blood ya see there!"

Goal Setting for Nordic Skiers

I've never taken New Year's resolutions too seriously. Often, it seems to me, folks make resolutions that are unrealistic or impossible to evaluate, and almost inevitably, a few days or weeks into the new year, the old habits reemerge.

Athletes and coaches are very experienced at making and keeping resolutions, only they think of it as setting goals. Everyone, from Little Leaguers to Olympic champions, has set goals and strived to achieve them. But successful goal setting is more complicated than it might first appear. To begin with, a worthy goal must be a reach. If the objective is easily accomplished, it is probably not a worthy goal. On the other hand, there must be a reasonable chance of achieving the objective. A target that is too lofty might actually create a sense of discouragement rather than inspiration toward reaching the target.

One solution to this dilemma is to establish multiple goals: perhaps short-term, intermediate, and career or lifetime goals. A worthy short-term goal might be to get some quality exercise at least five days each week. This would support an intermediate goal of finishing in the top 25 percent of your age group in a local road race, while your lifetime goal might be simply to maintain your body weight, cholesterol and blood pressure at healthy levels.

One helpful tip for establishing goals is to avoid the temptation of linking your objective to someone else's performance. For those of us who routinely compete in sporting events, it doesn't take long to recognize the hotshot in your age group who typically takes home the hardware. It's very tempting to succumb to the temptation of thinking, *If I could just beat 'ol What's His Name, I know I'd be doing well.* A better approach would be to figure out how fast a pace it would take, on a typical day, to finish ahead of the hotshot, and build your goal around achieving that pace.

One of the things experienced athletes learn to recognize is that life frequently interferes with training plans. Sickness, family obligations and the unpredictable nature of the weather often throw a monkey wrench into the best-made plans. It is important to remember that you established your goals as guideposts for your journey toward health or athletic success, and if necessary, you can adjust them.

After a decade of coaching the male Nordic skiers at Dartmouth, I wrote a book that illuminated the five areas that I felt a promising athlete must address to reach full potential. Since then, I have been gratified by the feedback the book generated, not only from skiers but from coaches of other sports and even from non-athletes.

The first requirement of Nordic skiing success is physical fitness. To excel at cross-country skiing or biathlon, you must be in shape. Physical conditioning is a science in its own right, but in simple terms, a successful athlete must have a balance of explosive, muscular power and aerobic endurance.

Nearly as important as conditioning is skiing technique, the ability to use that power effectively to move over the snow toward the finish line. This category was complicated back in the 1980s by the addition of the skating technique to the sport of cross-country.

Since Nordic skiing has long been recognized internationally as the most demanding of endurance sports (as evidenced by the consistently top oxygen-uptake testing scores by skiers), it follows that the fuel used to generate all that energy output might be important. Through the years, nutrition has gained more and more significance in the development of top athletes and the achievement of championship performances.

Equipment and waxing are important components to success in skiing. During recent decades, technological advances in ski construction, base structuring, and waxing breakthroughs have created significant performance improvements.

Finally, there is the area of sports psychology or mental preparation. In my estimation, this is the area about which the least is known, yet, I believe, holds the secrets to the most outstanding improvements. Regardless of the sport, if we think back to truly remarkable performances like Joan Benoit's 1984 Olympic Marathon victory, Bill Koch's 1976 silver medal, or the 1980 U.S. Hockey Team's "Miracle on Ice," the deciding factor is rarely better conditioning, technique, equipment, or food, but instead, some inner fire, a mental desire that overpowered self-doubt and allowed the athletes to perform their best.

Now, back to those New Year's resolutions: no more desserts, less TV and more exercise...

Celebrate Winter

The Dunkin' Donut Challenge

Today any capable coach recognizes the contribution of sound nutrition to athletic performance. But this wisdom has only recently become widespread. When I coached the Dartmouth Ski Team, my greatest nutritional challenge seemed to be keeping those hard-working cross-country skiers filled up. Because of time and budget constraints, we would frequently stop at fast-food restaurants. My fourteen athletes could put away more food at one McDonald's stop than an entire busload of leaf peepers. A typical skier's order sounded like this: "I'll have two Big Macs, a large fries, a chocolate shake...oh, and a fish fillet, an apple pie, and a large glass of water. Thanks!" I have no doubt the magnitude of our orders earned several teenage food servers recognition as "employee of the century."

Once, when I was taking the team to Quebec for a training camp, we stopped in Drummondville for supper. After descending on the local McDonald's with the efficiency of a swarm of locusts, we waddled back to the van to resume our drive north. As I pulled into traffic, one of the skiers burst out, "Hey look, there's a Dunkin' Donuts! Let's get some for the road!" I slammed on the brakes in disbelief.

"You've got to be kidding! How could you eat any donuts after what you just put away at McDonald's?"

"Easy."

The team captain's voice rose above the chorus, "I could eat a dozen donuts by myself, right now, no problem!"

I swerved into the Dunkin' Donuts parking lot and came to a stop in front of the plate glass window, which displayed rows of sugar-coated, glazed, jelly-filled, and chocolate-covered concoctions. I turned to the captain with a smile and said, "You're on! I'll buy you a dozen donuts just to see you eat them! But if you can't finish them all, you pay."

I was certain they would back down, but a lively discussion followed. A couple of the seniors confidently maintained they could do it and one of the freshmen chimed in, "Yeah, me too, no sweat."

Someone from the back of the van announced with a flourish, "The Drummondville Dunkin' Donut Challenge is about to commence!" There was considerable debate as to how difficult it would be to eat a dozen BUCKWHEAT donuts, but everyone finally agreed the jelly-filled, pink-frosted, Christmas Specials would be more of a challenge. For the next 20 miles the skiers debated rules. They finally agreed that the goal was to eat a dozen donuts, after a normal MacDonald's meal, within a forty-minute time limit, and to whistle, demonstrating that you've swallowed the last one. By this time, I was having severe misgivings. Was this something a prudent and responsible parent would endorse? I doubted it. I gave them my "everything in moderation" speech, to no avail. They listened politely, but soon after I finished, the self-appointed announcer reviewed the rules and introduced the contestants.

Even though two seniors instigated the Challenge, as the contest unfolded, attention was focused on two freshmen. Tom Longstreth and Tim Derrick roomed together, trained together, and were both over 6-foot-2, and thus became known as the Twin Towers. After generating excitement over the event, the upperclassmen cleverly manipulated Tim and Tom into a donut duel, so to speak. Complete with an official timekeeper, a competition jury to settle disputes, designated coaches for each contestant, and an announcer providing the play-by-play, the competition began.

For several minutes I watched in the rearview mirror as the Twin Towers happily munched donuts. Longstreth was the first to show signs of strain. Even though it was bitter cold outside, he opened a window and leaned his face into the freezing air. He was working on donut number eleven when he plaintively mumbled, "Could you pull the van over for a minute?"

He assured us he wasn't sick, but just needed some air and a chance to stretch his legs. Meanwhile, Derrick quietly continued eating. As Longstreth paced beside the van in the freezing Quebec wind, a weak whistle sounded from a rear seat. Derrick had done it! One dozen candy-covered donuts, after a full meal, in less than forty minutes! Even the seniors were impressed. Amid slaps on the back and congratulations, Tim calmly reached for Tom's remaining donut.

"Just so none one thinks I had trouble with the first dozen," he said, finishing off number thirteen.

That first donut challenge took place a long time ago, and those college athletes are now prudent adults: businessmen, lawyers, educators, and medical doctors. They still share a love of Nordic skiing and, surprisingly, a passion for good nutrition. But the Dartmouth Nordic skiers still go to Quebec for preseason training, and I understand they still stop in Drummondville. The power of tradition is a frightening thing.

Celebrate Winter

The Art and Magic of Waxing Cross-Country Skis

Perhaps the most intriguing aspect of cross-country skiing is the art of waxing. Before the skating technique, a basic knowledge of waxing was essential to the enjoyment of the sport. The goal was simple: from the wide assortment of waxes available, find the combination that would provide the greatest forward glide over the snow, yet at the same time ensure firm grip for striding down the track and climbing hills. This challenge was compounded by changing weather and variable snow conditions. Anyone who skied in the old days (before waxless bases), has horror stories about wet, heavy snow, frozen to the running surface, making gliding impossible, or of skis so slick that only agonizing effort by aching arms on the poles brought the unfortunate skier back home. For coaches, waxing is frequently a nightmare, since racers often blame a poor performance on bad wax, but seldom give a good wax job the credit for a victory. After a couple of decades of ski coaching, I have several vivid memories of races that were influenced by waxing.

Perhaps my worst waxing blunder came during my rookie year of coaching at Dartmouth. My predecessors, Al Merrill and Jim Page, had both been legendary coaches. Al was known as "The Silver Fox," partly due to his distinctive white hair but mostly because of his uncanny ability to "hit the wax." Early that season the U.S. National Championships were held at Waterville Valley, New Hampshire. This was before the skating revolution, and the new-fallen, wet snow made the waxing horrendous. Waterville's racing trail included quite a bit of flat skiing on a golf course before heading up into the woods for a 2-kilometer climb, followed by a long, thigh-burning downhill. I was frantically putting every conceivable concoction on the Dartmouth team's practice skis, telling the guys, "Go try 'em. Make sure you test 'em in the woods, then come back and tell me how they work."

Moments later my returning skiers announced breathlessly, "The U.S. Ski Team is using red and silver klister."

"What about these test skis?" I asked.

"Slipped, no kick at all!"

"Did you try 'em the woods?" I asked.

"Didn't have time," they answered.

It was minutes before the start. Nothing I had tested worked well on the glazed tracks of the golf course, but I was afraid the snow in the woods would be drier and have a tendency to ice up. As the seconds ticked by, the guys became more insistent on what they had heard the U.S. Team was using, so we set up an assembly line and began applying the sticky, red and silver combination. As the early racers left the starting gate, I was still torching skis and burning my thumb in hot klister.

I managed to scramble out to a strategic turn at the bottom of the long descent as the leaders came through. You could have described the location as "The Coaches Corner" since most of the U.S. Team, college, and club coaches were standing there. With the start list in hand and anxious glances at my watch, I tried to interpolate from the early competitors when my Dartmouth guys should be coming into view. Minutes crept by without a trace of a green uniform. Finally, my first Dartmouth skier appeared: red-faced, sweating profusely, and double-poling laboriously where others had coasted around the corner. I ran along the track offering encouragement. Eyes straight ahead, struggling on, the skier ignored me. As he rounded the corner, something made me ask, "How's the wax?"

Now, that got his attention! He almost stopped, turned his beet-red face over his shoulder, glared at me, and shouted with conviction, "IT STINKS!"

There were nervous chuckles from the gallery of coaches on the corner, and one of my colleagues asked in a deadpan voice, "So Morty, how do you like college coaching so far?"

The worst of it was, I had to stand there for the next 45 minutes while the rest of my sixteen skiers hobbled past. Ironically, that race served as my initiation into the informal fraternity of Nordic ski coaches since, at one time or another, we have all badly bungled the wax.

Of course, there have been some rewarding memories over the years as well (although they seem to be as much about psychology as they are about waxing). I've seldom (if ever) done anything intentionally dishonest, even during the intensity of a national or international competition. But I've come pretty close to stepping over that line a couple of times where waxing is concerned.

I believe waxing is an important part of cross-country racing and that skillful waxers have earned a significant advantage over those who are less experienced. In 1974 Ronny Yeager was one of the top cross-country competitors in the U.S. He was a tough, scrappy athlete from Durango, Colorado, who rode bulls in the rodeo for summer training. He was a veteran of several National Championships and two years later would go on to anchor the 1976 Olympic relay team to an impressive sixth-place finish. Training high in the Rockies, he had an awesome VO_2 uptake, the most impressive of all the national team athletes at the time (including Bill Koch).

But Yeager radiated insecurity about waxing. He would dance around from one athlete to another, nervously gathering information. Some of his teammates coolly ignored him, some actively avoided him, while others blatantly lied to him. I couldn't bring myself to lie, but it was irritating that he couldn't rely on his own judgment, especially during early-season races that were used for team selection.

Prior to each race in one series of competitions, he repeatedly asked me to compare skis on a gentle downhill section of the course. The purpose of this ritual was to confirm that his skis were as fast or faster than mine. The accepted procedure was to scratch a mark with the tip of a ski pole in the snow beside the track and align your bindings with the mark; then, from a standing start, break your skis loose, assume a tuck position, and glide until you coasted to a stop about a hundred meters down the track. Then you stepped to the side of the track so that the next skier (if he had faster wax) could glide past in his tuck. Rarely did gliding distance differ by more than a few inches.

By the third race in the series, I was tired of these wax tests and devised an innovative method to put an end to them. When Ronny approached me as usual, I politely declined. He insisted, so I reluctantly agreed. At the designated downhill, I said, "You go first, I'll be right behind you."

He marked the starting point in the snow, lifted his poles, and as he gathered speed, compressed into a tuck. Before he came to a stop down the track, I lined my bindings up with his mark, and leaned into the strongest double-pole I could manage. Ronnie had coasted to a stop and stepped out of the track as I glided by, still in my tuck. His jaw dropped in disbelief. He made me repeat the test, which produced the same results.

As luck would have it, the race that day was an interval start and I was seeded 30 seconds behind Yeager. In the previous events of the series, he had been battling Bill Koch and Tim Caldwell for first place. That day he was well back; in fact, I passed him and went on to finish fourth overall. I'm certain that Yeager was so convinced that his skis were slow, he expected me to overtake him. It wasn't long, of course, before Ronny caught on and stopped seeking me out before races to test wax. I also suspect the experience helped him generate more confidence in his own waxing instincts. At any rate, he had an impressive career on the U.S. Ski Team until the lure of the rodeo commanded all of his attention.

A similar situation developed when I was coaching the Alaska delegation to the 1977 Junior National Cross-Country Championships, held that year in Fairbanks. Waxing in Fairbanks is probably the most straightforward in the nation, even in March. Just rub on the coldest wax you've got! But coaches are often more competitive than their athletes, and in the days prior to the first race, coaches from across the U.S. and Canada were gliding repeatedly down sections of the track to determine the fastest wax.

I had noticed by then that people have loyalties to specific waxes and will try to win glide tests simply to demonstrate the superiority of their favorite. To eliminate this favoritism among our coaches, I numbered the test skis (rather than label them with the wax that was being tested) and gave each skier a wooden tongue depressor, numbered to correspond with the pair of skis which he rode. On a clipboard I kept the code, recording that pair #4 was waxed with Rode Green, pair #6 was Swix Special Green, and so on. We started our tests from precisely the same point each time on a slight downhill, and marked where we stopped with the tongue depressors. Since ski lengths differ, it is customary to mark both of these points next to the toe of the boot.

As the races approached, I knew we had a psychological advantage on the visiting teams. As the hosts, we were familiar with the trails and more accustomed to the snow conditions. More than once, after we had finished our wax testing, I had noticed other coaches carefully identifying our starting mark in the snow beside the track, gliding down the hill, and comparing how they fared against our test skis. I decided to make it easy for them (sort of).

On the final day of training before the first championship race, I marked a tongue depressor "START," and put it in the snow. But I told all my coaches to line the tips of their skis with the starting point rather than the bindings. I also asked them to mark their point of furthest glide by placing their numbered tongue depressor next to their ski tip. When we finished our tests, I left the markers in the snow. Before long, visiting racers and coaches were testing their skis against our markers: all falling short because they were starting with the binding (rather than the ski tip) next to the marker.

Our wax during that week of racing in Fairbanks was as good as anyone else's (perhaps better than some) but what really made a difference was that most of the other coaches and athletes were convinced that we had some secret concoction, available only to the Alaskans, which was giving us a tremendous advantage. The Alaskan team did have a wonderfully successful championship—their finest in many years—but it was not due to any secret wax. It was due mostly to psychology.

While waxing or ski preparation can have a significant impact on performance, especially in extreme snow conditions (warm or cold), I suspect most races are won by athletes who have the confidence, determination and mental toughness that they expect to win.

Celebrate Winter

The Drama of Choosing an Olympic Team

We just have to acknowledge at the outset that selecting athletes to represent the U.S. at the Olympic Games is an imperfect science. In some sports, like ice dancing for example, the decision is largely subjective — the opinion of judges — while in other sports, like track and field, the criteria are objective — minutes and seconds or feet and inches.

It's trickier for endurance sports like cross-country skiing and biathlon. With athletes whose systematic preparation takes years, it is widely recognized that "peaking" for the Olympics is essential to achieve that elusive, "best-ever" performance. But for most American endurance athletes, earning a spot on the Olympic team is a necessary interim step toward competing at the Games. For some, if they don't peak at the tryouts, there will be no opportunity to compete in the Games.

And biathlon is especially unpredictable. At the trials held in Fort Kent, Maine, to select the athletes who would represent the U.S. in Torino, weather played a significant role in at least two of the four days of racing. The opening events, a 15 kilometer for women and a 20 kilometer for men, were contested in a freezing rain that made it difficult to see the targets.

Many of the favorites faltered, leaving the door open for less experienced competitors to earn valuable points. The women's race was won by Denise Teela of Anchorage, Alaska, in just her third year of competition. Jacob Beste, of Minneapolis, who was forced to abandon the second half of the 2004/2005 World Cup competitions due to illness, redeemed himself by winning the men's event. Veterans of the 2002 Salt Lake Olympics, Jeremy Teela and Rachel Steer, were uncharacteristically far back.

The following day, a cold front brought blizzard conditions, a strong north wind and heavily falling snow. Athletes squinted through the swirling snowflakes to see their targets and bent against the gusts as they struggled for the finish line. Anchorage's Rachel Steer used her experience to win the women's sprint, while recent UVM graduate Lowell Bailey topped the men's field.

After a two-day rest break over the New Year's holiday, the competitions resumed under nearly ideal conditions. The women's pursuit format competition was won by Sarah Konrad from Laramie, Wyoming. A 1989 graduate of Dartmouth, Sarah got serious about Nordic skiing after college, eventually earning spots on both U.S. cross-country and biathlon teams to the 2005 World Championships. Tim Burke of Paul Smiths, New York, and a longtime training buddy of Lowell Bailey took the men's race.

January third, the final race of the series dawned clear, still, and cold. By midmorning, in the bright sunlight, the temperature had inched up enough to permit the scheduled start, but spectators and race officials were bundled like the Michelin man. Tension in the stadium was evident as the competition got underway. With the best-three-out-of-four selection procedure, the athletes who were still "in the hunt" knew what they had to do to make the team. The seasoned veterans, Jeremy Teela and Rachel Steer, knew what was required, and had enough physical reserves following a week of tough competition to lead their fields. Jeremy's wife, Denise, and Jacob Beste, who had won the first races, were far back.

There was anxiety, elation and disappointment as points were calculated, double-checked, and eventually the Olympic Team was announced. As expected, Rachel Steer led the women. She was joined by the twins, Tracy and Lanny Barnes from Durango, Colorado, and Dartmouth skiers Sarah Konrad and Carolyn Treacy, a native of Duluth, Minnesota.

Four men joined Alaskan Jay Hakkinen, who was preselected for the Olympic Team thanks to an impressive six top-twenty-five World Cup finishes. Those four men were Tim Burke, Jeremy Teela, Lowell Bailey, and Brian Olsen from Minneapolis.

Days after the team was named, they were headed to Europe for World Cup competitions in Ruhpolding, Germany, and Antholz, Italy. Then to drive across northern Italy to the Torino Olympic Biathlon venue at Cesana San Sicario. Were they primed for "best ever" performances at the Games, in front of the world?

Celebrate Winter

Lake Placid, 1980

In the summer of 1978, with some misgivings, I accepted the position of head coach of men's skiing at Dartmouth College in Hanover, New Hampshire. My hesitation arose from the fact that my late wife and I both loved living in Alaska, I enjoyed teaching and coaching at Dimond High School in Anchorage, and after four years of skiing for Middlebury, I had severe misgivings about working for the enemy. But both Mimi and I had family in New England, and several skiing buddies had assured me that the Dartmouth job was one of the best ski coaching positions in the nation, so we packed up and moved to Thetford, Vermont, less than a 20-minute commute to Hanover.

My first winter was rough. My predecessor, Jim Page, was a Dartmouth grad and a Nordic combined Olympian, and had coached the Big Green skiers to an NCAA Championship in 1976. Several of his skiers were understandably frustrated that he left. I had big shoes to fill. Adding to my challenges was the fact that after more than two centuries of educating men, Dartmouth had gone co-ed in 1972, and six years later was still fighting to establish equal opportunities for its women undergraduates. Having spent the previous ten years in Alaska, I was successful in recruiting several highly talented skiers, both male and female, to Dartmouth. But those Alaskans were accustomed to training together and were not happy about separate programs at Dartmouth.

My second winter at Dartmouth, 1979–1980, began cold but delivered little snow. My boss, Al Merrill, who ran the Outdoor Programs department, had been recruited to oversee the Nordic events of the 1980 Winter Olympics, nearly four hours northwest of Hanover. This was a tremendous tribute to Al and to Dartmouth, but unfortunately some administrators at the college were concerned about the amount of time he was spending at Lake Placid versus in Hanover. In fact, the Lake Placid Games were facing a crisis due to an unprecedented lack of natural snow. Faced with cancelling the Nordic events of the Olympic Games, Al made the courageous decision to attempt to cover the Nordic ski trails with machine-made snow (which had never before been attempted) and hold the events as planned. In the face of opposition and even ridicule from European Nordic authorities, Al and his devoted crew of volunteers made the snow, trucked it out on the course, groomed it with big Sno-Cats and held the Olympic events on schedule.

But prior to the Games, I received a call from the president of the U.S. Biathlon Association, Howard Buxton, who also happened to be a general in the Vermont National Guard. Apparently, the head coach, a recently retired national team member, was having a tough time with three of the six competitors named to the Olympic team. Since three of the 1980 Olympic biathlon team had been teammates of mine in 1976 and a fourth member of the Lake Placid team was a Dartmouth grad, Howard thought that as a last-minute addition to the staff as an assistant coach, I might be able to defuse what was quickly becoming a volatile situation. I told Howard that it was unlikely I would be permitted the time away from my duties at Dartmouth for a couple of reasons: first, we were in the midst of the competitive ski season, and second, it was clear that Al Merrill was taking heat from the college's administration for the time he was away from campus in Lake Placid. Howard's response to my concerns was simply, "If I can get the administration to approve your absence, how soon could you be in Lake Placid?" An hour later, he marched into my office at the college in his army, class A uniform, adorned with service ribbons, gleaming brass, spit-polished shoes and the general's stars on his shoulders. "Pack your bags," he said with the hint of a smile.

"How did you pull that off?" I asked.

"I just told the Dean that you were essential to the national priority of hosting a successful Winter Olympics. I also think the uniform helped."

Lake Placid is a small resort community nestled in New York's Adirondack Mountains. It was probably an ideal location for the 1932 Winter Olympics, but the scope of the Games had changed dramatically in 48 years. In an effort to minimize anticipated traffic snarls, all spectators, volunteers and those without official credentials were required to park in a huge, frozen field in Keene Valley to be bussed the remaining dozen miles to Lake Placid. Unfortunately, the bus schedule was unreliable until well into the Games, and in that vast parking field I encountered distraught spectators with tickets to Olympic events but no transportation to reach the events in time. The small village was also stretched to its limit providing accommodations for the athletes, volunteers, officials, press and spectators. Since I was a last-minute addition to the biathlon coaching staff, I ended up sharing a motel room with the elderly father of the U.S. biathlon team leader, Peter Lahdenpera. I learned later that my roommate had been a hero of the Finnish resistance during the 1939 Winter War against the Soviet Union, and an invaluable advisor to the architects of the famous Tenth Mountain Division.

The Opening Ceremonies were held in a temporary stadium, on a broad field not far from the ski jumps, just south of town. The weather cooperated with a clear cold day that emphasized the colorful clothing of the athletes as they marched in, the lighting of the flame and the several large, hot air balloons that drifted over the crowd. Years later, I learned that one of my college ski teammates, after serving in Vietnam, became head of flight operations for the FBI. In that role he was responsible for part of the security at the Lake Placid Opening Ceremony. He told me that during the event there were four helicopters in the air (but out of sight below the ridgelines of the surrounding mountains), ready to respond instantly to any potentially dangerous incident.

1980 was a tough year for U.S. Nordic skiers and biathletes. To begin with, the public assumed that competing at Lake Placid provided our athletes with a valuable home-court advantage. Actually, it was almost the opposite. Following Bill Koch's remarkable, silver-medal performance four years earlier at Innsbruck, the press and Nordic enthusiasts simply assumed that a gold medal was in his future, especially with the Games in the USA. But at that time, U.S. Nordic skiers were more accustomed to training and competing in relative obscurity. The attention and notoriety had a negative rather than positive effect on our athletes. Since the trails at Mount Van Hoevenberg had been constructed for the 1980 Games, the U.S. athletes hadn't skied them that much more than the Europeans. Jet lag wasn't a factor since most of the foreign athletes arrived on site two weeks before the competitions. And for the biathletes, everyone was still adjusting to the switch from shooting large-caliber rifles on a 150-meter range to shooting .22s at 50 meters. Before the conversion, our Remington .223s were widely regarded the most accurate rifles on the circuit (providing us a bit of an advantage). Following the conversion, almost everyone switched to Anschutz .22s, and any advantage we might have had disappeared.

Following the traditional schedule, the men's 30 kilometer was the first Nordic event following the opening ceremonies. It might have been pressure from the relentless, unrealistic expectations of the press, or missing the wax on the machine-made snow, or simply having an off day, but partway through the race, Bill Koch knew he was well off the pace and simply abandoned the course in frustration. There was a flurry of confusion and concern when he failed to appear at the finish line, but that was eventually resolved. Stan Dunklee had the top U.S. result in the event with thirtieth place. These were not the results that the American press and Nordic fans were expecting.

In an innovative attempt to reduce the staggering costs of hosting an Olympic Games, the Lake Placid Organizing Committee collaborated with the New York State Department of Corrections to build and use the Ray Brook Correctional Facility as the Olympic Athletes' Village for the duration of the Games. The entire complex was constructed of concrete blocks, the rooms were small, and the single window in each room was a narrow, vertical slit in the wall. Security at the Ray Brook Olympic Village was strict, with metal detectors and physical inspections of backpacks and duffels at every entry of the facility. Biathletes had an additional security check. While they were allowed to take their rifles to their rooms to be cleaned or for dry firing in the evenings, the bolts to the rifles remained at the security checkpoint in a locked and guarded cabinet. Ray Brook is about eight miles north of Lake Placid, and Mount Van Hoevenberg, the site of the Nordic skiing events, was another eight miles south of the village. This meant that the athletes staying in the Olympic Village had to anticipate significant delays in clearing security and traveling to their competition venue for training or a race.

This somewhat arduous routine sabotaged one of the relatively high-strung U.S. biathletes in his first Olympic competition, the 20-kilometer individual race. Arriving at Van Hoevenberg, he realized to his horror that he had neglected to retrieve the bolt to his rifle from the security cabinet, back at Ray Brook. It was quickly determined that there was not enough time before his start to drive back to Ray Brook and return with the bolt. Although the U.S. team always travels with a spare rifle, athletes frequently customize their personal rifles to fit their physiques and shooting positions. While the unfortunate athlete should have been warming up, testing his skis and zeroing his rifle, he was frantically scrambling around the venue trying to find an available bolt that would fit his Anschutz rifle. Moments before his start, he found a compatible bolt, but by then he was virtually exhausted by the pre-race anxiety. He finished in forty-fifth place with 21 minutes shooting penalty added to his ski time. The Soviet who won the event shot clean.

Leaving the biathlon venue one day late in the Games, I ran into my Soviet friend, Alexander Tikhonov. He was waiting for a shuttle bus back to Ray Brook, his rifle casually slung over his shoulder and a cigarette in his mouth. I was shocked and I let him know it. He shook his head in what I perceived as discouragement. "Finished competition...No more sportsman." During his international biathlon career, Tikhonov had been Soviet national champion more than thirty times, and he had accumulated more than a dozen Olympic and World Championship medals. But for some quirk of fate, in four Winter Olympic Games, he had failed to win a single individual gold medal. The Alexander Tikhonov I saw briefly in Lake Placid knew that his biathlon career was over, and in spite of a chest full of medals, he had fallen short of the ultimate Olympic goal.

The American press had also put a tremendous amount of pressure on Eric Heiden, who was expected to medal in all five speed-skating events for men. This was unprecedented since the 500-meter and the 10,000-meter speed-skating events are often compared to the 100-yard dash and the marathon in track, typically attracting sprinters and distance athletes, respectively. After the first week of the Games, it became apparent that the press and the public would be disappointed if Heiden won four golds and a silver. But in spite of a couple minor scares, Heiden persevered, and his fifth medal ceremony seemed to have attracted everyone in upstate New York. In another nostalgic touch, which might have been a nod to the 1932 Games, the medal ceremonies were held each evening on the frozen surface of Mirror Lake. Thankfully, the weather had been cold, and the ice was probably plenty thick, but I doubt the Organizing Committee anticipated the attendants that showed up to celebrate Heiden's accomplishment. As I joined the throng approaching the podium, placed well out from the shore, I was next to a man in a big ABC-TV parka. Just then, the ice released an audible crack, not uncommon in cold temperatures. Looking at the dense crowd ahead of us surrounding the podium, I asked, "How much weight do you think this ice can support?"

"Good question," he responded as he stopped, letting others push ahead to get closer to the podium. "I guess I can see well enough from here."

I stopped there as well, and as others continued to flow past, I imagined the chaotic scene of the ice collapsing under the huge crowd, hundreds flailing helplessly in the frozen water and Eric Heiden's remarkable Olympic achievement overshadowed by a colossal Olympic tragedy. Fortunately, my anxiety was unfounded, the medal ceremony went off without a hitch, Heiden received the enthusiastic celebration he deserved, and aside from a bit of ominous groaning, the ice remained firm.

By late in the Games, the mood of the U.S. biathletes and coaching staff was in the pits, in spite of Lyle Nelson breaking the top twenty in the 10-kilometer sprint and the U.S. relay team finishing a respectable eighth place. Several of the athletes were sick and everyone was exhausted. As cells opened up at the Ray Brook Correctional Facility (Olympic Village), I was relocated from the motel room I had shared with Col. Lahdenpera to be closer to the athletes. One evening as several of us quietly ate dinner, an Olympic Committee official approached our table.

"Hey guys, I have several complementary tickets to tonight's hockey game. Who's interested?"

Tired, sick and discouraged, the athletes at our table scarcely acknowledged the offer. Feeling a little embarrassed, I asked our group, "Isn't anyone interested in a hockey game?"

"I'm too tired," was one response.

"I've had it with the security check points," was another.

"Too many bus rides, I'm going to my room and read."

Feeling sorry for the USOC official, I said, "Well, if you're really trying to get rid of them, I'll take one."

"Here you go, but you'd better get moving if you want to catch the start."

The small group of us from Ray Brook joined the throng filing into the new arena in Lake Placid moments before the game began, not even knowing who was playing. It turned out to be USA against the Soviet Union. At the time, nobody gave the scrappy Americans much of a chance against the dominant Russians who had defeated the NHL All-Stars 10–3 in an exhibition game before the Olympics began. Three days before the Opening Ceremonies, the Soviets defeated the U.S. Olympic hockey team 13–0 in a practice game. There was little doubt that we were going to be beaten, the question was how badly.

The Olympic arena was packed with loud, enthusiastic hockey fans. In the first period, the Soviets demonstrated the cool, disciplined poise that had led them to several previous Olympic and World Championship gold medals. But the USA's goalie, Jim Craig, kept denying the Soviets' shots, and as the first period ended, the score was a surprising 2–1 for the Russians. Then, as the buzzer was about to sound, Mark Johnson tied the score. I remember glancing from the goal to the clock to see if the period had expired before the shot went in, then erupting with the crowd when the tie score remained on the board. At that point, most of us who had had doubts about the U.S. team realized that although a victory over the powerful Soviet team might not be in the cards, we certainly weren't seeing the blowout we had feared.

The second period was similar to the first—crisp, disciplined playmaking and shots by the Russians; scrappy, determined defense by the U.S. and remarkable saves by Jim Craig. At the end of the second period, it was 3–2 for the Soviet Union.

The third period was a white-knuckle blur because by then the entire arena knew that a remarkable upset was possible. Mark Johnson scored the tying goal, and then miraculously, Mike Eruzione slapped in the go-ahead score. The remaining minutes of the game seemed endless, since we had the fear that somehow the Russians would come alive, tie the game then pull ahead. But as the seconds ticked away, everyone in the packed arena was on their feet, shouting, chanting and stamping. We were in the balcony and could feel the floor flex with the stamping.

At the buzzer, there was pandemonium on the ice as the U.S. players buried Jim Craig. The unabated celebration spread from the ice to the stands, where weeping fans hugged total strangers. I was puzzled to spot U.S. coach, Herb Brooks, survey the scene from the team's box, then turn and exit under the stands. I learned later that he felt the athletes deserved the credit for the victory, and he didn't want to detract from that. I also noticed the Soviet team, lined up on their end of the rink, waiting for the customary, post-game fist bump with the opposing team. As the U.S. celebration continued, I wondered if our athletes would have had that discipline and composure had the outcome been reversed. Eventually, someone remembered the other team and the U.S. players straggled past the shell-shocked Soviets.

That evening, Lake Placid's Main Street, which had been closed to traffic, was a sea of Olympic athletes, fans, officials and volunteers, all of whom were still smiling, hugging and celebrating what announcer Al Michaels had aptly described as "The Miracle on Ice." I knew at the time it was probably the greatest sporting event I would ever see.

Sometimes the Excitement Is Traveling to or from the Race

Without a doubt, my worst nightmares during eleven years of ski coaching at Dartmouth College involved heavily loaded vans and icy New England roads. Although we had our share of near misses, thankfully we were never involved in an accident. Three memorable incidents involving transportation to skiing events are still vivid in my memory.

I think it was the winter of '79–'80 and there had been almost no snow throughout the Northeast before Christmas. Our normal, pre-season, Nordic training camp had been postponed, relocated, modified to dry land, and finally canceled. The situation hadn't improved much after Christmas, but Terry Aldrich, head coach of skiing at Middlebury College, had found a pocket of good skiing near Old Forge, New York. He spread the word, and the eastern college teams congregated there for a few days of training and a couple of low-key time trials.

As we headed home after several days of hard skiing in the Adirondacks, it finally began to snow. I was tired, the van was heavily loaded, and snow was accumulating on the road, normal winter driving conditions for a ski coach. A glance in the rearview mirror revealed a van full of exhausted, snoring athletes. We were descending a long, gradual hill somewhere near Lake George, when the road twisted away to the left. I turned the steering wheel, but the van continued straight, on an oblique course for the snowbank and guard rail on our right. I gently pumped the brakes to no effect. I remember calmly mumbling to my sleeping passengers, "Hold on, boys, we're going in," and bracing myself for the imminent crunch of the guard rail along the length of our van.

Like some master magician's trick, we simply disappeared into a "poof" of snow, as the loaded van bashed through the roadside bank. No scraping along the guardrail! No crunch of metal! We just floated silently through the snow. I came back to my senses and realized we were plowing through a roadside rest area, blanketed by more than a foot of new powder. Even with all the manpower I had in the van, pushing the heavy vehicle out would not be easy.

Before we floated to a stop, I cranked the steering wheel back toward the highway and accelerated. My timing was perfect. Without skidding or spinning the wheels, we bulldozed across the parking lot, bashed back through the snowbank again, and reemerged on the slippery pavement.

I resumed breathing several minutes down the road and stole another glance in the rearview mirror at my passengers. This time they were bolt upright, wide awake, eyes huge with disbelief. I tried to sound casual, "I just thought you guys might need to stop for a pee. I didn't notice until we pulled in that it was closed for the season."

Someone from the back of the van deadpanned, "We didn't need to go *THAT* bad."

Mark Ford coached the men's Alpine team at Dartmouth. Mark quickly developed a reputation as an extremely conscientious and meticulous coach. I often watched him study waxing charts and thermometers between runs of giant slalom, trying to determine whether the conditions had changed enough to re-wax. The athletes would try desperately to convince him that the wax was great, hoping to avoid the hassle and stress of re-waxing and scraping between runs.

Mark was just as disciplined after a race, carefully checking the result board for disqualifications, protests, or mathematical errors. The athletes, on the other hand, had done their thing and were eager to get back to Dartmouth.

At a major Alpine competition in North Conway, New Hampshire, Mark was deep in a discussion with race officials inside the base lodge, but within sight of his van, which was already loaded with skiers. His racers became increasingly impatient, but they couldn't get his attention. Finally, Ken Graham (the team's undisputed practical joke champion) took over. He had all the skiers crouch on the floor out of sight. Then he locked all the doors. The van was parked in a sloping lot in front of the lodge. Ken scrunched down in the driver's seat, released the parking brake, pushed in the clutch, and allowed the van to slowly...start...rolling.

That got Mark's attention fast (along with everyone else's in the building). He bolted from the base lodge, sprinted to the rolling van, and dove for the door handle — only to find it locked! Just before Mark tore the door off the van, Kenny appeared, grinning from the driver's seat, and brought the van to a stop, inches from disaster.

I never got a full report on the atmosphere in the van during the ride back to Hanover, but I do know that Mark didn't return to the lodge to finish his conversation.

The Putney Relays were one of the most enjoyable Nordic competitions in the East for decades. During the years that John Caldwell was the coach of the U.S. Ski Team, there were always plenty of hotshots to race against, and even though the Relays fell on a Sunday after one of the major collegiate winter carnivals, the college teams were usually well represented.

My sophomore year at Middlebury, I was invited by teammates John Brodhead and Bobby Nields to join them for the Putney Relays. The three of us drove to Putney through a blinding snowstorm in John's Volkswagen bug. Because of the weather, we arrived late and didn't have enough time to test wax. Nieldsy smeared one type of klister on his right ski, another variety on the left, and headed out to warm up. He returned minutes before the start, out of breath and sweating. Earlier he had agreed to ski the lead-off leg of our relay team.

"How's the wax?" Brodhead asked.

"Well," Nieldsy stammered as he struggled with his warmups and starting bib, "the right one is slippery as hell, and the left one wants to ice up!"

"What're you going to do?" I asked, worried about getting something to work for my second leg of the relay.

"Hell, I'm going to go with them; I figure I got a kicker and a glider, what more do I need?"

In spite of Nieldsy's innovative new technique, we won that year's Putney Relay, earning giant cans of Caldwell's maple syrup and beautiful silver belt buckles. We were a tired but happy trio as John pulled the VW onto the Interstate for the drive back to Middlebury. It was still snowing hard, so before easing from the access ramp onto the highway itself, John rolled down the bug's frosted side window to check the traffic.

What happened next was like something out of a surrealistic movie — an explosion of white! Brodhead and Nieldsy, both sitting in front, were literally buried in snow! In the rear, I was covered to my waist. John was gasping for breath. When he turned around, his thick glasses were still on his face, but behind them was a solid layer of snow making him look like a character from "Little Orphan Annie." Then we heard the huge, Highway Department snowplow rumbling down the Interstate.

John had rolled down his window at the instant the snowplow roared past, power-packing several cubic yards of wet snow into the VW. Once John cleared the snow from behind his glasses, it took us several minutes to shovel out the car. It was a cold, wet ride back to Middlebury, but I've always been grateful that John stopped to take a look before pulling out onto the Interstate.

Ecstasy and Agony in Bozeman

The 1985 Eastern Intercollegiate ski season was an emotional roller coaster that only intensified as the team traveled to Bozeman, Montana, for the NCAA championships. Through a combination of successful recruiting, hard work, and excellent coaching by Mark Ford, Dartmouth's Alpine team was the best in the East. In spite of jet lag, altitude, and soft, western, spring snow, the Dartmouth racers were the team to beat at Bridger Bowl, in the mountains just north of Bozeman. In the opening event, the giant slalom, the men were superb, placing first as a team. The real fireworks came from feisty Tom Foote, a sparkplug of a sophomore who carved his way to the individual gold medal. At the finish line, the Dartmouth skiers were euphoric. Earning both individual and team victories was a great way to open the championship!

Amid the excitement and laughter at the finish line, I noticed a pained look on Footie's face. In a quiet moment, I asked if he was okay.

"Yeah," he groaned, "just a wicked pain in my stomach. Probably nerves. I was really up for this one."

After the excitement abated and the van was loaded for the drive back to the motel in Bozeman, Footie lost his lunch in the parking lot. Amid the ongoing teasing about his victory and his case of nerves, Mark and I both watched him carefully.

Tom did not have a good night, and by morning it was clear he should be checked by a doctor. Since it was a race day for cross-country, Mark said he would take care of Footie before the Alpine skiers returned to Bridger for slalom training. About noon, as the cross-country race was winding down, an announcement over the loudspeaker called me to race headquarters. One of the event officials put an arm on my shoulder and steered me away from a crowd of spectators and the press.

"You've got a problem, Coach. Tom Foote is in the Bozeman hospital with acute appendicitis, but will not allow the doctors to operate. They say his condition is serious and it's getting worse by the minute. You'd better get right down there."

Moments later, as I sped from the mountains back to Bozeman, I imagined the possible headlines: DARTMOUTH NCAA SKI CHAMP DIES ON OPERATING TABLE DUE TO COACH'S NEGLIGENCE.

The corridor outside Footie's room was filled with scowling nurses and angry doctors. The biggest member of the group, a guy in green operating scrubs with a mask hanging below his chin, looked like he could have played defensive tackle on any NFL team. He grabbed me as I tried to slip into Footie's room.

"You his coach?" he demanded.

"Yes, I am," I answered, surprised by the vice-like grip on my arm.

"Well let me tell you something, Buster! That's one very sick kid in there. That appendix could burst at any time, and when it does, it will be one hell of a mess! I'm going to give you about two minutes to talk some sense into him, before I wash my hands of this whole screwed up situation. You got that, Coach?"

"Yes, Doctor!" I answered, heading into the room.

Footie didn't look too bad to me. He was sitting up in bed, reading comfortably. He had had similar stomach pains before and assured me that they had always gone away. He wasn't eager to go under the knife without good reason. A knee operation the previous summer had resulted in a slow and painful recovery.

I tactfully suggested a second opinion and ran the gauntlet of the surgical team in the hallway a second time to locate a doctor who had been recommended by Dartmouth alums living in Bozeman. When I found the doc, he graciously agreed to follow me back to Footie's room for a diagnosis. As we walked the long, sparkling halls together, he smiled reassuringly.

"You know, Coach, there is one very, reliable method of diagnosing appendicitis. If you press your hand steadily and firmly on the patient's right abdomen, then release the pressure suddenly, the pain of appendicitis will launch the patient through the roof."

As we entered Footie's room, the doctor nodded to the O.R. staff still waiting in the hall. The doctor spent several minutes chatting with Tom about the race, skiing in the West, and his college major. At the same time, he was conducting a general examination: checking Tom's pulse, peering down his throat, looking into his eyes. Only after minutes of this easygoing conversation and superficial inspection did he pull down the sheets and begin to gently palpate Tom's abdomen. The doctor casually glanced at me as he increased the pressure on the right side of Tom's stomach. When the doc released his hand, Tom's yell could be heard halfway to Bridger Bowl. The doctor put his hand on the athlete's shoulder and said convincingly, "Tom, you have acute appendicitis, no question about it! The best thing for us to do is get it out of there right away."

Still recoiling from the pain, Tom mumbled, "Okay, okay, okay."

Within 30 seconds the surgical team was in the room, handing me forms to sign, slathering Tom's stomach with shaving cream, and manhandling him to a rolling table. The NFL surgeon gave me a stern look and grunted, "You stay here," as he followed his patient down the hall.

I sat in the empty hospital room wondering what I would tell Tom's parents if the surgeons opened up their son and found a perfectly normal appendix. I was halfway through a two-page *Reader's Digest* article when the big surgeon pushed through the door. Something must have gone wrong! He had been gone 10 minutes, at the most!

"Everything's okay," he reassured me. "Damn good thing we didn't screw around anymore though. We got it in the nick of time! He'll be sleeping for a while, and we'll keep him in here for a day or so, but he'll be fine."

"Thanks a lot, Doctor. I appreciate your patience with us. Sorry it took so long to get the go ahead."

"No sweat. I just figured you hot-shot Easterners didn't want some Montana cowboy cutting into your national champion! I don't blame you, you've had so few of 'em." He smiled for the first time and headed down the hall.

The third day of competition at Bridger Bowl was the slalom, and Dartmouth was riding high. In addition to the individual and team victories in the giant slalom, everyone was relieved that Footie would be okay. Jory Macomber was primed! It was his senior year, and he was Alpine co-captain and one of the strongest slalom skiers in the East. His first run was blistering, the fastest on the course. But a slalom victory takes two runs, and at the NCAA's everyone goes for broke. There would be no cooling it on the second run to protect his lead. The deeply rutted spring snow was tricky for Easterners, but Jory was the epitome of quiet confidence and determination.

He attacked the second run with the same assurance and power that led to his impressive first run. As the entire Dartmouth contingent held its breath, silently chanting, "He's gonna do it, he's gonna do it," Jory rocketed through the bottom half of the course. He was nearly home when, two gates from the finish, he hooked a ski tip on a gate, and sprawled headlong across the snow. It was devastating. None of us could comprehend that it was over. To have skied so brilliantly for more than 60 gates and lose it all two gates from the finish...

It took me several minutes to recover from the horrible, gut-wrenching, empty feeling that consumed me. Then I saw Jory standing alone several hundred yards below the finish. He wasn't throwing his poles into the woods in frustration, too often the case with disappointed ski racers. He was just standing by himself, his back to the course, looking at the magnificent skyline of Bridger Bowl.

Helping an athlete through the intense discouragement of a bitter defeat is one of the most difficult and delicate challenges of coaching. Often, in our own insecurity, we coaches say too much. I skied up to Jory, put an arm around his shoulders and gave a squeeze. Jory nodded a silent acknowledgment, as tears streamed down his face.

In my mind, Dartmouth Skiing had two national champions in 1985. Tom Foote skied one of the most brilliant giant slalom races of his impressive career and quite simply "blew the socks off" his competition. Jory Macomber, through his quiet leadership and inspiring Winter Carnival results throughout the season, convinced his teammates that they could win at the NCAA's. But what took even greater leadership and maturity was ignoring his personal disappointment in the slalom to celebrate the overall team success. There are many ways to define a champion.

One of the Rewards of Coaching

Coaching high school or collegiate athletes can be stressful, exhausting and incredibly time consuming. Unless you are coaching one of the revenue-producing sports (football or basketball) at a major university, the financial compensation is nothing to brag about. And there is virtually no job security; one or two losing seasons, perhaps due to fluke injuries to key team members, and the coach may be looking for a new job.

The rewards of coaching, especially a "minor" sport like skiing, are more intangible. One of the most gratifying is the opportunity to work with eager, motivated students at a time in their athletic development when they are capable of the most dramatic improvement. There is tremendous satisfaction in coaching an inexperienced but determined high school or college freshman into a varsity letter winner by senior year. I was privileged to enjoy this experience during five years of coaching high school runners and skiers in Anchorage, Alaska, and eleven years of coaching Nordic skiers at Dartmouth College.

But in the years since I gave up coaching, yet another even more significant reward has emerged: observing what my former athletes have done with their lives. Not surprisingly, the competitive zeal and work ethic of the endurance athlete is still evident, regardless of the career path. These were high school and college students who were driven to do their best, both in the classroom and in sports, so it is little wonder that they excel in their professions as well. Two excellent examples are Tom Longstreth and Max Cobb, who both made their homes in Vermont as adults.

Tom Longstreth arrived at Dartmouth College from New York City, looking more like a lanky basketball player than a Nordic skier. But what he lacked in experience on snow he made up for in quiet, unassuming dedication. By his junior year, he was challenging skiers who had been winning races since junior high school, and by his senior season, Tom was a regular on the six-man Winter Carnival team. Twenty-five years out of college, Tom (or Stretch, as he was known to his Dartmouth teammates) continued to race well in local and regional Nordic events, including the annual Craftsbury Marathon.

But Tom's most significant achievements since college have not been on skis. Always an activist for the disadvantaged and underprivileged, Tom followed several years of working with Vermont's Youth Conservation Corps by earning a master's degree in public policy from Harvard's Kennedy School. He then returned to Vermont in 1996 to lead Recycle North, an innovative program in Burlington with a three-pronged mission: first, to accept unwanted household appliances, thus keeping them out of our overflowing landfills; second, to teach unemployed people the skills needed to repair the discarded appliances, in the process giving them the confidence and training to become productive members of the community; and third, to operate a store in which the repaired appliances and other household items are sold at very reasonable prices. Since he took over, the programs have expanded, include four sites, and the organization is now known as ReSOURCE.

Max Cobb arrived at Dartmouth from Cambridge, Massachusetts, via Proctor Academy, where he developed a love for Nordic skiing and the outdoors. As a freshman, Max claimed the dubious distinction of being responsible for a team helmet policy, since he fell so frequently on roller skis it was determined that he (and everyone else) should be required to wear helmets during those workouts. Yet by his junior year, Max was guiding his Dartmouth teammate, Joe Walsh, to a medal in the blind category of the Disabled World Skiing Championships. Two years later, the pair won Paralympic bronze at the 1988 Games in Innsbruck, Austria.

That taste of international competition prompted Max to accept a position with the U.S. Biathlon Association as the domestic race coordinator, where he quickly learned the essentials of the sport. A year later, when the association hired a couple of European Olympians as coaches, Max was promoted to assist them. Through the following years he waxed skis, drove vans, made travel arrangements, scheduled training camps and coordinated with the Olympic Committee. When Salt Lake City won the bid to host the 2002 Winter Olympics, Max Cobb was the unanimous choice for the vital position of chief of competition. The success of those events catapulted Max to leadership positions within the U.S. Biathlon Association and, even more impressively, in the International Biathlon Union.

Both Max and Tom continue to demonstrate the quiet determination that distinguished them as college skiers, but now their efforts benefit their communities and beyond.

Celebrate Winter

Dipping the Flag

I've been a member of six Winter Olympic teams. As the team leader for the U.S. biathletes, my responsibilities were pretty mundane: I attended meetings, disseminated information to the coaches, ensured that our competitors were properly entered in their events, and occasionally ran interference for the athletes with the media. But due to the worldwide fascination with the Olympics, every team leader endures the actual sixteen days of the Games trying to suppress a constant sense of panic.

At the 1972 Summer Games in Munich, two American sprinters, both potential medal winners, watched their qualifying heats on television, unaware of a last-minute schedule change. Their team leader has lived with the guilt of that oversight ever since. There are dozens of similar horror stories.

One of my worst nightmares as biathlon team leader occurred at the Calgary Olympics in 1988. Lyle Nelson had been selected by his teammates to be the flag bearer, to lead the entire U.S. delegation into the Opening Ceremony while the entire world watched. It was a tremendous honor, and Lyle was a worthy choice. For many years he had been the top U.S. biathlete, he was a West Point graduate, and Calgary marked his fourth Winter Olympics as a competitor. Lyle's selection as flag bearer also provided an intense focus of media attention on the biathlon team. For an obscure sport, this was a public relations gold mine.

Finally, the afternoon of the Opening Ceremony arrived, blown in by a bitter Arctic wind roaring across the Alberta plains. As the parade of nations was about to begin, Lyle, carrying the impressive Stars and Stripes, cornered me near the back of the U.S. delegation.

"Hey Morty," he said brightly, "I've been thinking about dipping the flag."

According to Olympic tradition, the flag bearers of each nation dip their flags to the dignitaries of the host country in a gesture of respect and good will. But in the 1936 Winter Olympics in Garmisch, Germany, the American athletes decided to snub Hitler by refusing to dip the Stars and Stripes as the U.S. Team marched past his reviewing stand. The snub was repeated in Berlin the following summer, and has become an American tradition at every Olympics since.

Lyle continued: "The Canadians are neighbors and strong allies. They've spared no expense to make this the best Winter Olympics ever. Why shouldn't I dip the flag to acknowledge their hard work and their friendship? Isn't that what the Olympics Games are all about?"

My mind became a tornado of conflicting thoughts. Philosophically, I agreed with Lyle, the Olympics should be above national politics. But I could also imagine the feeding frenzy that the unauthorized break with tradition might stir up in the media, and among some of the crusty, old-timers on the Olympic Committee. Before the ceremony was over, all the positive exposure biathlon had achieved in the past few days could easily be replaced by hate mail.

The parade was about to begin as I responded. "Lyle, I agree with you. I don't see how it diminishes our standing in the eyes of the world if we dip our flag to the Canadians. You were selected to carry the flag, so you follow your conscience. I'll back you up, whatever you decide."

Lyle smiled and returned to the front of the delegation as we began marching into the stadium. The roar of the crowd was deafening. My pulse was pounding, mostly from anticipating the international incident I had just sanctioned. As we circled the huge stadium, I strained to watch the flag, but the throng of waving athletes ahead of me made it impossible.

It wasn't until we boarded the buses much later that I was able to catch up with Lyle. "Well, did you dip the flag?" I wanted to prepare for the media onslaught that almost certainly would follow.

Lyle's face broke into a broad grin.

"You know, it was funny. I'd finally made up my mind to do it, but I got so distracted by the excitement, all the cheering, the music, and the TV cameras in my face, that I forgot to look for the reviewing stand. By the time I spotted it, we had already marched past, and it seemed stupid to dip it then."

I tried to act nonchalant. As a U.S. citizen, I strongly endorsed the gesture of respect and friendship, but as the team leader who would have been responsible, I'm mighty glad Lyle got caught up in the celebration.

Passing the Torch in Canmore

Perhaps the most significant symbol of the Olympic Movement is the Olympic flame. Although it is just one of the rituals that have become a part of the Opening Ceremony, the lighting of the Olympic flame seems to capture emotions like nothing else. By the Calgary Winter Olympics in 1988, the coast-to-coast torch run had become a national event in itself. Eighty-nine days before the start of the Games in Alberta, the Olympic flame arrived in Newfoundland and began an 18,000-kilometer journey through all the Canadian provinces. The torch was carried by 6,500 Canadians of all ages and from all walks of life. They transported the flame on foot, by snowmachine, on dogsled, and even by wheelchair. On February 13, more than two hundred thousand people jammed the streets of Calgary to cheer the flame on to McMahon Stadium, where sixty thousand more endured bone-chilling cold to witness its arrival.

The torch was carried into the stadium by two of Canada's former Olympic heroes, Alpine skier Ken Reed and speed skater Cathy Priestner. Holding the flame aloft between them, they circled the stadium and approached the stairs to the cauldron. Then, to everyone's surprise, they passed the heavy torch to twelve-year-old Robyn Perry, who represented the youth of the world. Smiling all the way, she bounded to the very top of the stadium, reached high above her head, and tipped the torch into the huge cauldron, as thousands of spectators roared their approval.

A day later, in the mountain village of Canmore, two hours west of Calgary, I was discouraged. The magic of the Opening Ceremony had given way to the frustrating realities of my job as biathlon team leader. A couple of our athletes were fighting the flu, the press had begun its relentless pursuit of our top performer, Josh Thompson, and there had been harsh words between two members of our coaching staff. The Games were not yet a day old, and already I was up to my ears in alligators.

Sensing my discouragement, U.S. Biathlon's executive director, Jed Williamson, suggested we take a break from the stress of the Athlete's Village by walking to downtown Canmore, about a mile away.

"Come on, John, they're supposed to be running the torch through town on its way up to the Nordic Center. If we get to Main Street in time, we might get a good look as it goes by."

With several problems confronting me, I reluctantly agreed to join Jed. As we approached Main Street, we could see a throng lining the sidewalk. When we were close enough, we asked a bystander if the torch runners were approaching.

"They're already here," an enthusiastic woman responded, pulling us into the crowd for a better look.

I'll never know whether it was part of the plan or if some magnanimous torchbearer simply wanted to include the townspeople in the pageantry, but the official, Olympic torch was slowly making its way up Main Street, handed reverently from one spectator to the next. The brightly uniformed runners were walking beside the line of citizens, keeping pace with the torch's progress. There was no cheering or shouting. Hundreds of people simply stood in quiet awe of the Olympic flame.

Jed and I remained where the woman had pulled us into the crowd, but as the torch approached, I was afraid we had unintentionally stumbled in the midst of a solemn ritual reserved for the host country, or perhaps just the residents of Canmore. When the Canadian woman sensed my concern, she said, "Stay put! You guys are on an Olympic team, for crying out loud."

Moments later the torch was handed to Jed. He looked into the golden flame as he turned, smiled, and held the torch out to me. It was heavy. I could smell the fuel oil and feel its heat on my face. I tried to take in the detail of the intricate metalwork that held the flame, and the delicate carving on the wooden handle. In an instant, I was passing it on to the generous woman who had pulled us into the crowd.

It was a powerful moment. Even after six Winter Olympics, it is one of the experiences I remember most vividly. To actually hold the Olympic flame put me in touch with the magnificent history of the Games, and to pass the torch on...well, that's what the Olympics are really all about.

Gloria

Nordic skiing lost a strong ally when Gloria Chadwick succumbed to cancer. Her own competitive background was in Alpine skiing, and later she managed two different Alpine ski resorts. But in my view, Gloria made her most significant contribution as an advocate for U.S. Nordic competitors at the Winter Olympic Games.

After various administrative positions within the ski industry, Gloria found her niche with the U.S. Olympic Committee. She served the USOC for almost a decade, opening and managing three Olympic Training Centers. The athletes who lived and trained at those facilities became part of Gloria's family. She would abandon her office at the Lake Placid Training Center to watch some of her "kids" practice at the ice arena, or drive out to Mount Van Hoevenberg's bobsled run to check on her "boys," most of whom were over six feet tall and weighed more than two hundred pounds.

At the last three Winter Games she attended, Gloria was sort of a den mother for American athletes and coaches at the Olympic Village. Her motto was simply, "Whatever's best for the athletes." A typical example of her philosophy occurred during an inspection visit of the Nordic facilities prior to the Albertville Olympics. We had been wined and dined in lavish French style by the man who would serve as mayor of the Athletes' Village. He apologized for construction delays, and acknowledged the considerable stress caused by the disintegration of the Soviet Union, which made it impossible for him to predict the number of athletes from new nations he would be obligated to accommodate.

I felt sorry for the mayor, squeezed between budget constraints, construction delays, and the uncertainty of world politics. But Gloria showed no mercy! She made it clear how many rooms the U.S. delegation required, and even specified which rooms she wanted. I worried that Gloria was being too demanding, but when the Games began in February and several new nations arrived unannounced, putting a severe strain on the Olympic Village, the U.S. athletes escaped the housing crunch because of Gloria's foresight.

It was at Calgary in 1988 however, when Gloria first converted me into a loyal fan. Canmore, the beautiful mountain village where the Nordic skiing events were held, was almost two hours west of Calgary. One afternoon early in the Games, Gloria received a directive from USOC headquarters in the city. The Jeep-Eagle dealers of America had scheduled an annual sales meeting in Lake Louise, a couple of hours northwest of Canmore. In addition to providing dozens of brand-new Jeep vehicles to the Winter Olympic team, these businessmen had made a contribution of $1 million to the USOC. Gloria's instructions were to recruit some Olympic team members, and drive them to Lake Louise for a banquet with the Jeep-Eagle dealers, and their boss, Lee Iococca. After a little arm twisting, Gloria found an athlete who wanted to go. Then she cornered a couple of coaches and a team leader, all of whom were afraid to turn her down.

Decked out in our patriotic Olympic team uniforms, we headed north, with Gloria behind the wheel of her new Jeep Wagoneer. Then it started to snow. Before long we were driving through a full-blown, Rocky Mountain blizzard. One of the coaches offered to take a turn behind the wheel, but Gloria just laughed and kept driving through the wall of white.

Without warning, red taillights began slashing back and forth across the road ahead. A huge tractor-trailer fish-tailed out of control. Gloria calmly downshifted and aimed for the roadside. We burst through a snowdrift, a wave of white billowing over the hood and roof. Then Gloria calmly accelerated, and we plowed back up the embankment, returning to the pavement beyond the jack-knifed truck. There were a few seconds of white-knuckle terror, but as soon as we had returned the road, Gloria cheerfully announced, "That's the great thing about these Jeeps, that four-wheel drive is there when you need it!"

We arrived fashionably late to the banquet but were a big hit to have made it at all, considering the storm. We thanked the hundreds of Jeep-Eagle dealers from all over the U.S. for their generous support of the

Olympic effort, and we got to hear Lee Iococca give an inspiring pep talk to his national sales team. For me, that evening was one of the highlights of the Calgary Winter Olympics. I still have a vivid memory of a poised, confident, and determined Gloria Chadwick getting us safely to Lake Louise and then back to Canmore. Come to think of it, her service to the U.S. Olympic Committee was a lot like that Jeep's four-wheel drive. Gloria Chadwick was always there when they needed her.

Celebrate Winter

Roller Skiing Rural Vermont

The breathtaking natural beauty of October fills Vermont's country inns with guests, creates waiting lines at our restaurants, and clogs our back roads with leaf peepers. And, autumn also brings another hazard to our back roads: roller skiers.

Because of Vermont's rugged geography and its long, cold winters, the Green Mountain State is a mecca for cross-country skiers. Not only do thousands of Nordic enthusiasts visit each winter to experience some of the best cross-country skiing in North America, but Vermont produces more than her share of our nation's top racers. Every four years at the Winter Olympics, Vermonters compete against the world's best in the Nordic skiing events.

Jeff Hastings from Norwich was only a fraction of a point away from a bronze medal in ski jumping at the Sarajevo Games in '84, while Guilford's Bill Koch won America's first Olympic medal in Nordic skiing, with his second place finish in the men's 30-kilometer cross-country at Innsbruck in 1976.

Unlike basketball players or swimmers, who can train at their sport year round, when the snow melts in the spring, Vermont's Olympic Nordic hopefuls hang up their skis and make do with dryland training. Variety is not a bad thing, and summer conditioning usually includes weightlifting, cycling and hiking in the mountains. But when the leaves begin to turn, variety in training becomes less important than specificity, and roller skiing becomes a critical component of the Nordic skier's workout schedule.

As a training device, roller skis are not new. In the late 1960s a Finnish company attached wheels to their delicate wooden racing skis for use on the roads in the summer. The wheels had an internal ratchet that mimicked the traditional kick and glide of cross-country skiing on snow. But the bamboo ski poles of that era had aluminum tips that were useless on the rough asphalt, so roller skiing never quite caught on.

There have been significant technological improvements in roller skiing recently, several of which are thanks to a mechanical engineer from southern New Hampshire named Len Johnson. Through the years, Johnson has improved the design of roller skis to the point where his products are widely used, not only in this country, but in Scandinavia as well. Perhaps Johnson's most significant contribution is the development of an innovative and effective speed reducer, which permits Nordic skiers to confidently negotiate previously dangerous descents.

During the eleven years I coached the Dartmouth Ski Team, my worst fears focused on roller skiing. It was an essential aspect of fall training, and although I required the athletes to wear helmets and reflective vests, I never overcame the dread that one of them would end up in a ditch or swiped by a passing car. I couldn't help noticing with irony that the average motorist will wait patiently as a farm tractor slowly pulls a loaded hay wagon back to the barn. But if a handful of brightly clad, Olympic hopefuls on roller skis, laboring up the final pitch of a gut-busting, 4-mile climb, delay traffic even slightly, tempers sometimes flare, and angry words are exchanged.

I was prepared for the worst one autumn day as I supervised a dozen college roller skiers on a narrow Vermont road when a beat-up old pickup truck skidded to a stop in front of me. Anticipating a tongue lashing, I timidly approached the rugged, bearded driver.

"Judas Priest, I hope the guy who come up with that there Lycra made a million," the guy blurted out his window.

I was totally befuddled.

"Them skintight suits! The guy who invented that Lycra shuda got a gold medal."

Come to think of it, that driver had a good point. Maybe fit, young Olympic hopefuls add as much scenic beauty to Vermont's back roads as green pastures dotted with Holsteins or autumn maples aflame with crimson and gold.

Report from the Skunkworks

Anyone who followed the action during the 1992 Winter Olympics in Albertville, France, quickly recognized the intensity of the athletic competitions. The medal winners usually achieved their victories by hundredths of a second or by tiny fractions of a scoring point. But some of the most intense competition at the Olympics took place in the predawn darkness. In most of the skiing events, the skillful selection and application of waxes to the running surface of the ski can make the difference between a medal or the third page of the results. High in the alpine village of Les Saises, site of the Olympic biathlon and cross-country events, small groups of coaches silently made their way to a "village" of portable trailers that served as waxing rooms, adjacent to the race course. Long before Mount Blanc reflected the faint pink of the approaching dawn, coaches with headlamps would scurry around the gentle hillside designated as the wax testing area, setting up their electronic speed traps on ski tracks that they felt had just the right gradient to provide the perfect test. It was a competition within a competition, or more accurately, layer upon layer. If the lights were on in the U.S. trailer, our coaches busily waxing, when their counterparts from other nations arrived, it was a small psychological victory. If the Russians or the Germans crawled under the chain-link fence surrounding the test area in the predawn darkness only to find small American flags claiming the best track, it was another small victory.

Moments before the start of a race, when a U.S. athlete, glide-tested her skis down the first overpass on the racecourse and radioed back to the wax building, "Whatever you guys put on pair #3 is awesome! I just out-distanced the Italians and Norwegians by at least a meter!" — yet another small victory.

Because of the confined space and the routine use of new fluorocarbon waxes, the trailer took on a "Star Wars" appearance: smoke and vapors escaping from windows and doors, and voices muffled by Darth Vader–

type respirators. One morning, an Olympic Committee official stopped by for a look and dubbed the trailer the "Skunkworks."

Yet in the midst of this intense vortex of competition, generosity, international understanding, and friendship flourished. The athletes from the three "new" Baltic countries radiated pride as they competed under their own flags, even though their fledgling Olympic Committees could afford only the most basic equipment and minimal coaching support. Immediately prior to the men's 50-kilometer cross-country event, a worried Latvian coach approached an American coach.

With embarrassment, the Latvian explained that the temperature had risen beyond the range of his team's limited wax supply. His nation had one competitor entered in the race, and there would be little chance of even finishing 50 kilometers without the proper wax for the difficult snow conditions. Could the Americans help him, the Latvian asked?

Surrounded by thousands of dollars' worth of the latest fluorocarbon waxes, an American coach hesitated for only a few seconds. Although waxing secrets are among the most closely guarded in the ski world, the American could see the desperation on the Latvian's face, and sportsmanship overpowered nationalism. After a few sentences of explanation to the biathlon coaches in the "Skunkworks," everyone pitched in. Within minutes the Latvian was running for the start, his athletes' skis freshly waxed and race-ready.

More than three hours later, a jubilant Latvian coach and his exhausted but happy athlete returned to the "Skunkworks" to express their gratitude. Although the young racer had not been a threat to the medal winners and was totally ignored by the press, he was tremendously proud to have represented his new nation with dignity, and in the process achieve a personal best for 50 kilometers, in spite of very challenging snow conditions.

The spirit of international cooperation and sportsmanship was alive and well at the Winter Olympics.

Back to Zakopane

Many years ago, I was a brand-new lieutenant, assigned to the U.S. Biathlon Training Center at Fort Richardson, Alaska. For a small-town boy fresh out of Vermont's Middlebury College, it was equivalent to an assignment on the moon. But in 1969, the World Biathlon Championships were held in Zakopane, Poland, behind a very real "Iron Curtain." That was like being sent into the den of the fearsome Russian Bear.

We were in a serious mood flying into Krakow. A State Department briefing before our departure had assured us that the Polish Secret Police knew we were active military and would attempt to embarrass or even detain us. Descending through the clouds for our landing, a stern admonition came over the intercom: "Absolutely no photography permitted in the airport. Violators will have their cameras confiscated." (Welcome to Poland.)

As we taxied toward the terminal, I was struck by how gray everything looked—the buildings, the parked aircraft, and even the people. Passport control and the recovery of our baggage seemed to take hours. Sullen officials studied our documents, carefully checked photographs, then tossed them back at us with distaste. Finally, we were permitted to load our gear on a decrepit bus, engulfed in its own diesel fumes. Our route to Zakopane took us through the city. Aside from buses and military vehicles (all spewing clouds of black exhaust), there was little traffic on the wide streets.

As our bus paused at a stoplight, I noticed a vacant lot where several young soldiers were aiming their rifles at silhouette targets placed against a wall. The troops wore shallow, flared helmets, typical of Eastern European armies. But what really caught my attention were the targets at which they were aiming. The crisp, black, head-and-shoulders outline unmistakably represented the bulbous "steel pot" of the U.S. Army.

We stayed at the large, austere Sport Hotel. The rooms were cramped, the plumbing faulty, the wall-mounted radio never worked (except to produce a mysterious static at unpredictable intervals), and what were provided as bath towels would not have passed for dishrags in the U.S. The food was awful. By the end of our stay, we were served animal parts rarely seen on tables in our country. I was reminded of a Vermont humorist who, when asked if he liked tripe, responded, "We don't eat our critters *that* close."

The State Department had been right. Every time we left the hotel for a walk to town, a couple of thugs in trench coats followed. For amusement, we would sprint down side streets just to see our "tails" run. If we succeeded in losing them (as occasionally we did), they would be scowling in the lobby of the Sport Hotel upon our return.

But through the gray light of communist-imposed gloom, two shining moments stand out. The first occurred at the opening ceremonies of the World Championships. High above the balcony seats, completely surrounding the ice arena where we were assembled, were life-size, black-and-white photos of young athletes. Scanning the dozens of images, I whispered to our interpreter, "Who are they?" He answered solemnly. "They were winter sports national champions or Olympians...and all were killed in the Second World War." It took a moment to sink in as I studied the young faces. What would it be like for a small nation to lose so many of its young sports heroes? It was impossible to even guess.

The second event took place during the biathlon competitions. From the time biathlon had been adopted as a Winter Olympics sport in 1960, it had been dominated by the Soviet Union. The 1969 World Championships were no exception, with Russians taking the top two medals in the 20-kilometer individual event and beating the second-place Norwegians by more than six minutes in the relay. But in the junior men's individual race, a short scrappy Polish boy named Andrzej Rapacz fought his way to a silver medal and became an overnight sensation. The sun broke through the overcast, our Polish hosts became more friendly, and the one intelligible word in every street corner conversation seemed to be "Rapacz." It was as if the sullen Communist façade had been shattered, and the Poles celebrated this spunky kid's challenge to Soviet domination.

But Rapacz's medal was not my final memory of Poland in 1969. After the competitions, as we prepared to depart for Krakow, the hotel manager, red-faced and angry, jumped aboard our bus. An interpreter explained that there was a serious problem with room 207 and the athletes assigned to that room would not be permitted to leave. I had been in 207! Not moving from his seat, our team leader commanded, "Morton, you'd better go straighten it out. But make it fast. We can't hold this bus, or we'll miss the airplane!"

I sprinted back into the hotel, while the irate manager shouted and shook his fist. The second floor was littered with piles of dirty sheets. In front of 207, a maid shook three of the ragged little "dish cloths" in my face, making it clear that there should have been four. As they continued to scold in Polish, I flailed through the pile of soiled linen until I uncovered the missing towel. I tossed it at her, emphasizing the point by holding four fingers in her face, then bolted down the stairs to the bus. I will never know if it was an honest mistake by a conscientious maid or an orchestrated attempt to embarrass the Americans, but I left Poland in 1969 with no interest whatsoever in a return visit.

So when asked if I would serve as team leader for the American biathletes competing at the 1993 Winter World University Games in Zakopane, I had to think it over. My memories of Poland were all gray: gray snow from coal smoke and diesel fumes, gray calves' brains on a dinner plate, ragged gray towels in a shabby bathroom, and the dour, unfriendly Poles I remembered from the Biathlon World Championships. But so much had happened in that country since 1969.

My curiosity overcame my memories, and in late January I herded twelve college athletes and three coaches through the departure gate in Frankfurt for our Polish Airlines flight to Krakow. I had expected an ancient, Russian Tupelov (recycled after Aeroflot no longer found it airworthy). There would not be room for all our skis, rifles, wax boxes, and baggage, and whatever was left behind would probably disappear forever. My fears were unfounded. The Polish plane was a brand-new European Airbus. Our inflight meal (though perhaps not delicious) was significantly better than the hard candies and stale bread I recalled from my previous flight to Krakow.

In the dark, with a light rain falling, the Krakow airport appeared much as I had remembered it, but if the arrival terminal hadn't changed, the people inside certainly had. As I led the team through passport control, armed with the rifle permits, information about the University Games, and pockets full of trading pins, we were surrounded by heavy-set uniformed officials. Before I could dig the rifle permits out of my briefcase, they were smiling, shaking hands, and babbling about "Universiada" and "Zakopane."

The following afternoon we confronted our next challenge. Arriving in Zakopane we learned that there had been bare ground until recently, and with only a week until the start of the University Games, the organizers were working frantically to preserve what little snow they had. Though there was some snow on the ground, it was not enough to adequately cover the forest trails of the biathlon venue in the neighboring village of Kiry. I surveyed the scene with a mixture of admiration and frustration. Several rugged volunteers, who appeared to be local farmers, shoveled snow out of horse-drawn carts to cover the trails. There was little chance that we would be permitted to train, when they were going to such lengths to prepare for the competitions. Just then I noticed a short, solid, ruddy-faced man charging purposefully around the biathlon stadium, supervising the shovelers, and shouting instructions. I recognized him from twenty-four years earlier.

"Andrzej Rapacz!" I shouted.

He stopped and strode over to us. I introduced myself, then introduced Andrzej to the U.S. Team as the Polish Junior Champion who spoiled the Soviet sweep on this very range in 1969.

"Andrzej, can we shoot on the range this week?" The hand signals and body language resembled a game of charades.

"Absolute!" he responded with conviction.

"Morning or afternoon?" I asked.

"No problem!"

"Can we train on the trails?" (This was the question I was worried about. The trails were barely skiable on snow filthy from coal soot, evergreen needles, and horse manure.)

"Absolute! John, my friend...America okay!"

A day or so later, I was approached by a young man whose demeanor suggested efficiency and self-assurance.

"Mr. Morton? Hello, my name is Piotr, and I'll be your guide." He was dressed in black Levi's (authentic, button-fly 501's, he assured me), a black leather bomber jacket, and cowboy boots. He could easily have stepped off any college campus in the U.S., except for his distinctly British accent. Once when I commented on how many private cars I had seen compared to what I remembered from 1969, Piotr answered brightly, "Oh yes, and since democracy there are many more options available on our new Polskis. The most popular by far is the heated rear window...keeps the owner's hands warm, while he's pushing it!"

When the rest of the U.S. skaters and skiers arrived, Piotr went to work for the assistant chief of the delegation, and introduced me to our new "guide," Agnieszka. Like Piotr, she spoke flawless English with a British accent. Unlike Piotr, Agnieszka was very shy and gave the impression of a frightened rabbit, ready to bolt.

The temperature had risen, the snow was melting, and having trained several days at Kiry, I didn't want to wear out our welcome. I was wrestling with what to do with the team that would be beneficial to their training yet keep us out of the organizer's hair for at least a day.

"Well then, Mr. Morton, how can I be of assistance?" Agnieszka asked, sounding more like she came from London than Wroctaw, Poland. I put her right to work, locating a map of the mountains in the Zakopane area, getting a local expert to recommend a four-hour hike, arranging with the kitchen for sixteen bag lunches, and finally, listening to the weather forecast to ensure that we wouldn't be snowed in at the top of some peak. Despite our concerns, Agnieszka was intent on joining us, so the following day we set off on an unforgettable five-hour hike, high in the Tatras. Agnieszka had no problem keeping up, city boots, pocketbook, and all. By the end of the trip, the athletes had adopted her as an honorary team member and friend. It was only later that I discovered Agnieszka had never before been in the mountains, or even on a hike!

The opening ceremonies of the University Games were held on the outrun of the ski flying hill. More than fifty thousand spectators commonly turn out for the World Cup ski-jumping events in Zakopane, and on the evening of the opening ceremonies, the stadium was packed. More than one thousand athletes from forty-eight nations marched in behind their flags. We strained to see Lech Walesa as we approached the reviewing stand. He stood and waved as the teams paraded past. As the welcoming speeches droned on (translated into three languages), the falling snow inspired a couple of youthful spectators, and a few snowballs arched through the spotlights toward the assembled athletes. Almost instantly, a good natured, multi-national snowball fight erupted as the organizers looked on helplessly, and the television crews debated which aspect to the ceremony to cover.

When the snowball fight began to lose momentum, a group of U.S. athletes attempted to start a "wave" through the assembled teams on the outrun of the jump. After a few tentative efforts, the wave took hold, arms reaching into the snowstorm, followed closely by a hearty cheer. It took only a short time for the fifty thousand spectators to pick up the ritual, and this time the TV cameras swung away from the dignitaries to follow the excitement as it coursed through the huge crowd. I watched in amazement, the exuberance of this impressive gathering of Polish sports enthusiasts, and was struck by the contrast of the somber opening ceremonies I remembered from the ice arena twenty-four years earlier.

Once the competitive events of the University Games were under way, the work really began. There were biathlon races scheduled almost every day, which required predawn departures for the coaches to the wax room. By this time Agnieszka had us all speaking fluent Polish (at least a couple of phrases). "Ile to kosztuje" (how much is it?), got constant use by the athletes in the open-air market on Zakopane's main street. But the real "ice breaker" was "czy masz krewnych w Chicago?" (Do you have

I have no doubt that the Olympic movement will continue to grow and flourish. But at the 1994 Winter Games in Lillehammer, the Norwegians set a new standard for athletic excellence. They reminded us of the ties that bind us together as a global family. And for sixteen days they welcomed the world to their small, snowbound country, and made us all participants in an unforgettable Celebration of Winter.

Celebrate Winter

Of Scholar Athletes and Commencement at Dartmouth

Head coach of men's skiing at Dartmouth was a great job. I worked with very bright, highly motivated, young athletes who loved the outdoors as much as I do. But coaching at Dartmouth was not without its frustrations. Because the varsity ski team traveled a great deal for competitions, sometimes causing the skiers to miss classes, there was a relentless assault from several members of the faculty, that athletics detracted from the *true* purpose of higher education, namely academics.

I took issue with those faculty members for a couple of reasons. First of all, I was able to point out that the academic average of the varsity ski team was higher than the academic average of the entire student body, in spite of the time my skiers devoted to their sport and in spite of the classes that they missed. Secondly, I was impressed by the opportunities for off-campus experience that skiing provided through competitions all over North America, Europe, including events behind the Iron Curtain, and even Asia. Finally, after observing my young athletes for several years, I knew firsthand how much they learned about themselves and each other while striving for victory on the ski trails during their four years of harsh New England winters. I remember two instances where athletes I coached struggled to balance academics and skiing.

I met Glen Eberle at a summer training camp hosted by the Olympic Committee in Squaw Valley, California. He was a big, strong high school kid from McCall, Idaho, whose impressive skiing ability was matched by a strong academic transcript. He had never heard of Dartmouth College, and I worked hard convincing Glen and his parents that the East wasn't solid pavement from Montreal to Washington, DC. To my excitement, the easy-going cowboy arrived in Hanover as a freshman fifteen months later.

Since his high school in McCall didn't demand that students take a foreign language, Glen had to fulfill his requirement at Dartmouth from a standing start. Russian is generally considered one of the most challenging foreign languages for English speakers to learn, but the Biathlon Junior World Championships were scheduled for Minsk,

Belorussia, that winter, and I knew Glen was a sure bet for that team. I convinced him to take Russian so that he could communicate with the athletes, officials and spectators whom he would meet on that trip to a Soviet Union, which was, at that time still depicted as "The Evil Empire."

Through hard work and persistence, Glen earned a B during his first term of Russian, but when he sought permission from his professor (who no longer teaches at Dartmouth) to miss two weeks of class at the end of winter term to participate at the World Championships *in Russia*, she refused. In her view, missing two weeks of her class was inexcusable, regardless of the reason.

Glen competed in Minsk anyway, and got a D for the term in Russian. The following year he participated at the World University Games in Bulgaria, and finally, in 1984 at the Winter Olympics in Sarajevo, all while still an undergraduate at Dartmouth. I wonder if any of his classmates gained a more intimate and comprehensive view behind the Iron Curtain than did this Idaho cowboy, thanks to his athletic talent.

Willie Carow came to Dartmouth from the Putney School, where he excelled as a musician and a cross-country skier. It was not long before he was playing French horn in the Dartmouth Symphony Orchestra and competing on the varsity ski team. The two were not always compatible. I may have been seen as a hard-driving ski coach, but Efrain Guigui, the conductor of the orchestra, was widely regarded as a tyrannical perfectionist. I might have grumbled a little if Willie was late to a ski team workout, but we both knew Guigui could raise the roof off Spalding Auditorium if Willie was late to a D.S.O. rehearsal.

Somehow, we muddled through. By his senior year Willie was first French horn in the orchestra, and co-captain of the men's ski team. More than once that season we had to arrange special transportation to speed Willie from the finish line of a ski race in Stowe or Middlebury back to the Hopkins Center for a rehearsal or a concert. The Maestro and I maintained an uneasy truce regarding the talents of a very gifted student athlete.

A few years after he graduated, Willie earned a spot on the U.S. biathlon team to the Sarajevo Olympics. Because of a blizzard and the postponement of the glamor events, biathlon took center stage for a fleeting moment, and Willie Carow skied and shot his way to twentieth place in the 10-kilometer sprint on coast-to-coast TV. Only four Americans had previously broken the top twenty in Olympic biathlon competition, and only one male from the U.S. bettered Willie's '84 result in the three Winter Olympics that followed.

I was having lunch at the Hopkins Center Snack Bar when I heard the news, and I noticed that the Maestro was in his office. On a whim, I knocked and introduced myself, "Mr. Guigui, I wanted you to know that Willie Carow, the student we shared a few years ago, just finished twentieth at the Winter Olympics in Sarajevo, the top American in the event." The dynamic conductor sprang from his chair, "What? My Willie at the Olympics?"

As I recounted to Guigui the details of Willie's accomplishments in skiing, his eyes filled with tears, and when I left his office, he gave me a powerful hug.

It had been several years since I had witnessed a commencement at Dartmouth. I left my coaching job in 1989, before those graduating were freshmen. But it isn't every day that you get to see the president of the United States in person, so I decided to attend. As the rain drenched the crowd of spectators, I had severe misgivings about the wisdom of my decision. But finally the colorful ritual began, the rain let up, and I scanned the young faces as they marched past. The procession stalled, and a few feet away I spotted Cammy Myler, for almost a decade one of America's top luge competitors, a World Cup medalist and a three-time Olympian. I was so accustomed to seeing her in red, white, and blue that I almost missed her in the black cap and gown.

Later in the ceremony, when President Clinton was introduced, it was noted that he had been a Rhodes Scholar. Having been asked to write a few recommendations during my coaching tenure, I knew that selection as a Rhodes Scholar reflected excellence in athletics as well as academics. It is certainly no secret that the president was an avid foot runner. When the Winter Olympic team was invited to Washington after the

Lillehammer Games, the athletes who joined President Clinton for his morning run were surprised to discover that he was not just a casual jogger. In fact, it had become a significant status symbol within The Beltway to be photographed running with the president. What few people realize, however, is that the cameras were stationed during the first mile of the run, since many of his running partners had trouble keeping pace with him for the entire loop.

I thought his remarks to the graduating class were right on target: an honest appraisal of the worldwide challenges that they faced, yet optimistic and inspiring. I felt sorry for the valedictorian, Kristin Cobb, who was scheduled to follow President Clinton on the program a few moments later. I shouldn't have. A young woman who finishes first in her class at Dartmouth with a 3.99 grade-point average in biology and philosophy, and who captained the most successful Dartmouth women's cross-country running team in years, can probably hold her own in any situation. And she did. She captured the attention of her classmates, a stadium full of spectators, and the president of the United States. She spoke about the value of education in our society, and reminded us of the significance of music, the arts, and sports to the educational experience. She gave specific examples from her own Dartmouth career of how participation in sports stimulated and intensified her drive for academic success.

Thank you, Kristin Cobb, for reassuring student athletes of all ages that the path they have selected, though difficult, may ultimately be the most rewarding. And thank you President Clinton, for showing student athletes everywhere, by your example, the heights of influence and public service to which they may soar.

Team Leader

It seems impossible, since my memories of Lillehammer are still so vivid, but the Nagano Winter Olympic Games are nearly here. I served as Team Leader for the U.S. biathletes at the previous three Winter Olympics, but it was high time for someone else to fill that role, this year in Japan. In some ways I envy my replacement. The biathletes who earn a spot on this Olympic team will include some of the most gifted ever to represent the U.S. Stacy Wooley, a graduate of Stratton Mountain School and Dartmouth College, had three top-twenty finishes on last winter's World Cup circuit, in addition to a twelfth place at the World Championships. Another American woman, Rachel Steer, who left her home in Alaska to attend the University of Vermont and train for biathlon, surprised an international field of competitors by taking bronze and silver medals last February at the World University Games in Korea. Many of the women Rachel beat in that competition will be representing their nations in Nagano this February.

Perhaps America's most exciting recent result in biathlon was Jay Hakkinen's gold medal at the '97 Junior World Championships in Italy. Like Rachel, Jay is an Alaskan who came East to train for biathlon and attend UVM. Although Americans have participated in international biathlon competition for almost forty years at the time, Jay Hakkinen was our first and only individual World Champion.

But in spite of these talented athletes and their teammates, my replacement will have his hands full. One of his top priorities will be attempting to manage the media. U.S. biathletes train and compete in total obscurity for years, only to be blinded by the glare of publicity during the Olympic Games. The biathlon team leader will walk a tightrope, trying to use that window of media attention to promote the sport, thereby attracting talented young athletes and corporate sponsors; but he must do so in a way that will not distract the current athletes from achieving their best possible results at Nagano.

There will be agonizing decisions to make concerning who will actually compete. Each Olympic team names more athletes than available starting positions, thus ensuring alternates in the event of injury or illness. Everyone who makes an Olympic team has trained incredibly hard for years, simply to be chosen. But because they are such fierce competitors, just making the team is never enough. They all desperately want to race.

Often the young man who was unbeatable at the tryouts in December, has slipped past his competitive peak by mid-February, or the young woman who surprised everyone by barely making the team after Christmas, is out-performing the veterans in workouts on the Olympic course.

Even after these agonizing decisions are made, the official ritual of entering the competitors in each event can produce stomach ulcers. At the height of their careers in the 1980s, U.S. Alpine skiers Phil and Steve Mahre were potential medalists any time they raced. Once, their team leader mixed up their racing bibs, a mistake that was not revealed until after the race, when both skiers were disqualified.

But, ironically, at the Winter Olympics, that gathering of the world's healthiest and fittest, my replacement's greatest challenge as U.S. biathlon team leader could very well be...drinking. A genuine love of sport may be the common language at the Olympic Games, but among administrators, officials and volunteers, it seems to be alcohol that fuels the conversation. Since the athletes are competing, and the coaches are working, the international social obligations become the responsibility of the team leaders.

They attend receptions hosted by Olympic Committees, and cocktail parties to honor corporate sponsors. There is wine at lunch with the French, and aqua vitae after supper with the Norwegians. The team leader is expected to sing with the Germans as he drains tall steins of their beer, and toss back shots of vodka after midnight with the Russians. You can be certain that this winter, my replacement will become an authority on Japanese saki.

The truth is, I'm actually looking forward to watching the Nagano Games on TV and cutting way back on my alcohol consumption. I hope our athletes ski fast and shoot straight, and I hope their team leader doesn't forget his aspirin.

Some Friendly Coaching for Russia's President Medvedev

Stavicha, Presidente Medvedev! I empathize with your frustration regarding the performance of Russia's Olympians at the recent Vancouver Games. It was a bold move on your part to publicly demand the resignation of your nation's Olympic administrators. I can identify, since I was a competitor, and have ever since been involved in biathlon, the only Olympic sport in which the U.S. has yet to win a medal.

You are probably correct to clean house, but I doubt your Olympic problems will be cured by a simple change in personnel. In my view, your current state of affairs is a result of at least three major factors, none of which will be easily resolved. The first is the double challenge created by the dissolution of the Soviet Union. I remember speaking with one of my friends on the Soviet biathlon team back in the mid-1970s. He explained that the Olympics were relatively easy for him because, in those days, he only had to beat three of his Soviet teammates, a handful of Scandinavians and a couple of central Europeans. In contrast, with 120,000 registered biathlon competitors in the Soviet Union at that time, there were often dozens of other Soviets who might beat him at their national championships or Olympic tryouts. That changed dramatically in 1990 when competitors from the former Soviet republics of Latvia, Lithuania, Estonia, Ukraine, Belarus, Kazakhstan, and others no longer competed for the Soviet Union. Even worse, almost overnight they were competing against Russia.

Adding to the talent drain was the loss of hundreds of highly qualified coaches who had been the backbone of the Soviet sports dynasty. They took their knowledge and passion for sport to the nascent Olympic movements in their new nations. In addition to losing coaching talent to former Soviet states, the emergence of a democratic government in Moscow meant that many experienced coaches accepted offers to coach in the West. To a certain degree, we here in the U.S. owe at least some of our improved results in Nordic skiing to several former Russian coaches who have relocated to here.

Finally, I believe your results have slipped because drug testing at the Olympics has become more sophisticated. I suspect that unethical Russian athletes, coaches and sports doctors, all desperate to maintain the façade of international sporting dominance, some time ago succumbed to winning by whatever means it took, including illegal doping. Prior to the last Summer Olympics in Beijing and the recent Vancouver Games, dozens of cheaters were caught, an alarming number of them Russians.

President Medvedev, I applaud your public commitment to the Olympics, but the medal count is the wrong goal. If you lend your influence to the organizers of the 2014 Sochi Winter Games, insure that they are fair and well organized and that the natural beauty of that region is featured, and make certain that the hospitality and generosity of the Russian people is evident to visitors and television viewers, Sochi will be a tremendous success and no one will care about the medal count.

SKIING — A WAY OF LIFE

A Day on the Catamount Trail

The Catamount Trail is a unique 280-mile cross-country ski trail running the length of Vermont. Along its route the trail passes through or near twenty-one of Vermont's finest cross-country ski centers, as well as dozens of charming country inns and lodges. Making use of old logging roads, snowmobile trails, rugged wilderness paths cut by volunteers, and the beautifully groomed segments in the participating touring centers, the Catamount Trail offers an exciting Nordic skiing experience for people of all ability levels, from beginner to expert.

It was snowing hard when I arrived at the Bolton Valley Cross-Country Ski Center, a modest building reminiscent of a trapper's cabin, complete with gravel floor and wood-burning stove. I was greeted by Rosemary Shea, executive director of the Catamount Trail Association. In spite of the new snow and strong winds, we were preparing to set out on a 12-mile, backcountry ski tour through some of the most rugged and beautiful terrain in Vermont.

Outside, we stepped into our bindings and adjusted the straps on our ski poles. It had stopped snowing, but the wind whipped the fresh powder into drifts. Rosemary had warned me that the tour began with a long climb, and she hadn't exaggerated. For nearly an hour we trudged up through a hardwood forest that moaned in the wind and cracked with the cold. Three other skiers had left Bolton Valley ahead of us, so we conserved energy by following their tracks through the deep snow.

At Bryant Lodge, a cabin maintained for overnight campers in the warmer months, we stopped for a breather. One of the challenges of back-country ski touring is maintaining a comfortable body temperature. While we were climbing from Bolton Valley, my turtleneck, polar fleece vest, and nylon wind shell had kept me warm. But after resting only a few moments in the wind outside Bryant Lodge, we were both shivering and eager to get back on the trail.

We pushed up the mountain, following the tracks of the skiers who had preceded us. My touring skis had waxless bases that worked well in the soft new powder, but Rosemary's wax was slipping, so we stopped while she attached climbing skins to the bottoms of her skis. In the old days, Arctic explorers used strips of seal skin to provide grip in deep, cold snow. Modern skins are made of synthetics, but they serve the same purpose.

We left the Bolton Valley trail system and encountered a series of difficult switchbacks up the east face of Bolton Mountain. We had climbed to an elevation of 3,300 feet—1,300 feet above our starting point. It was remarkably silent, the huge mass of Bolton Mountain completely shielding us from the persistent wind. I could imagine a relaxing lunch overlooking the Waterbury Reservoir on a sunny day in March, but in the brittle cold of January, we gobbled sandwiches and slurped hot tea standing on our skis.

After lunch, the steady climbing gave way to a rolling traverse across the thickly wooded eastern face of Bolton Mountain. There were short herringbone climbs and abrupt twisting descents, made challenging by sculpted waves of drifted snow. During one of those quick turns, a vital piece on one of Rosemary's climbing skins snapped in the cold. Since the difficult assent was behind us, it was not a crisis, but instead a sobering reminder of how serious a broken ski or binding could be on such a remote section of the trail.

The sky was a clear, pale blue above the Worcester Range to the east. Rosemary pointed out the summit of Mount Hunger, where in 1984 the concept of the Catamount Trail was hatched. Steve Bushey, Ben Rose and Paul Jarris had been weathered in on the summit. As they shared a bottle of wine and waited for the storm to pass, Steve cajoled his friends to join him skiing the length of Vermont. As a graduate student in geography at McGill University, Steve had done work preparing an atlas of cross-country ski centers in Vermont. That project had convinced him that it would be possible to ski the length of the state, connecting many of those touring centers. He set about acquiring the permission of landowners along the proposed route, and after talking Rose and Jarris into joining him, the three skied what is now the Catamount Trail.

Rosemary and I began our descent into the Miller Brook watershed in Stowe and overtook the three skiers who had broken trail for the entire climb and traverse. We stopped for a moment to be friendly, but the lure of a 4-mile descent through unbroken powder was too much to resist. When the other skiers showed no eagerness to retain the lead, Rosemary pushed off through the drifts.

The real joy of skiing, the adrenalin-pumping exhilaration, comes from flying downhill over the snow. And what a descent we had! The waves of wind-blown powder covered a firm crust: nearly ideal back-country conditions. We zipped through stately old maples and birches, searching for the next Catamount Trail marker on a tree ahead. More than once we had to stop abruptly for a stream bubbling through the blanket of snow and ice.

At one crossing Rosemary noticed the unmistakable scars left by the claws of a large black bear in the bark of an old beech tree. We passed a sugarhouse and followed a stream that tumbled through granite boulders, shrouded in a thick curtain of ice.

We had been on our skis for almost four hours and we were tired, but it was almost a disappointment to reach the Nebraska Valley Road. We had descended 2,300 feet through untracked powder, a dream come true for any backcountry skier.

After a short walk on the Old Country Road, we put on our skis for the final climb to Russell Knoll and the groomed trails of the Trapp Family Lodge. The wind had died down and the sun was at our backs, filling the hardwood forest with sparkling golden snow between deep purple shadows. We climbed 400 feet out of the Nebraska Valley before we stepped onto the beautifully groomed tracks of the Trapp Family's trail system. Our backcountry skis felt clumsy on the packed surface. It seemed strange to see other skiers after several hours of almost total isolation.

We emerged from the woods to see the Trapp Family Lodge in the alpenglow just before the sun disappeared behind Mount Mansfield. Though nearly spent from five hours of challenging skiing, we were drawn to the touring center by the promise of a crackling fire, a hot drink, and one of Rosemary's favorite Nordic skiing rituals, chocolate.

It had not been an easy tour. We had climbed almost 2000 vertical feet and descended through wind-blown drifts. But it was a very pure form of the sport: no chairlifts, no snow guns, no trail-grooming machines. As the Worcester Range to the east slowly faded from a rich pink to a deep violet in the twilight, I had a wonderful feeling that we had experienced the sport as it was meant to be.

A Beautiful Day at the L.L.Bean Ski Festival

Many years ago, L.L.Bean, one of the most respected names in U.S. outdoor sporting goods, organized a winter sports festival in the scenic village of Bethel, Maine. The company invited suppliers of skis, snowshoes and snowboards to provide a selection of their latest products. Then, "Beans" recruited dozens of experienced instructors to teach eager participants how to master the new equipment. Hundreds of winter sports enthusiasts traveled from as far as Pennsylvania and Virginia to hone their skills, attend old fashioned church suppers, and in general, celebrate winter.

At the 1996 L.L.Bean Winter Sports Festival, I was instructing with Dorcas Wonsavage, a veteran of three U.S. Olympic cross-country teams, and one of the most flawless technical skiers in the nation. We enjoyed teaching together and found that our observations and methods meshed nicely. It was also a treat to be part of a staff of instructors that featured Bill Koch, at the time the only U.S. cross-country Olympic medalist and the 1982 World Cup Champion.

It was snowing hard Saturday morning when Dorcas and I met our students. We were disappointed that only a handful of people braved the storm for our session, titled "Classic Technique for the Competitor." But considering the unpredictability of recent New England winters, it was a joy just to be in deep, fresh snow.

As we led our little band across the fairways to our designated instruction area, we heard the clamor of youthful voices and were joined by an enthusiastic group of twenty-five junior high school racers. Suddenly, with more than thirty students of widely ranging abilities, Dorcas and I had our hands full. But many of our skiers made dramatic progress and the morning lesson sped past.

At noon, we grabbed a sandwich, then set up equipment for a demonstration of waxing techniques for cross-country racing. Waxing is considered by many to be an intimidating and mysterious aspect of

Nordic skiing. The participants who attended our clinic fired questions until it was time for the afternoon session on skating technique.

The junior high kids returned, rejuvenated by lunch and eager to learn the secrets of skating. It had stopped snowing, and a few more adults joined our class, but they seemed reserved, probably self-conscious about their technique in comparison to the rambunctious school kids. Even though it was a large group, displaying a wide range of skating experience, by hustling, Dorcas and I were able to work through the five basic skating techniques and address the dozens of questions that were asked by our students.

During a rest break, I gave the class a brief history of skating, including the key role that Bill Koch played in revolutionizing the sport. At three-thirty, the school kids and their teachers left to catch their bus home. Dorcas and I stood quietly with the remaining adults as the sun finally broke through, painting the low clouds gold and making the new powder sparkle like diamonds. We asked our skiers if they wanted to take the long way back to the inn, and they eagerly agreed.

Dorcas led, dancing over the snow like an elf. I trailed behind our group, skating beside a woman who had shown concentration and determination during the class. After asking me a couple of questions about her technique, she glanced over and blurted, "Hey, you're the one who wrote the book! *Eat to Win*, or something like that, wasn't it?"

"*Don't Look Back*," I gently corrected her.

"Right! I loved that book! And Dorcas is a three-time Olympian! When I signed up for this clinic, I never dreamed I'd be skiing with celebrities!"

We were approaching another group of students and I noticed their instructor was Bill Koch.

"Well, Susan," I responded, "you're about to ski past the *real* celebrity, right now!" Her shock at recognizing Bill was almost complete, and she struggled to maintain her composure as we skated by.

Further on, the rest of our group had stopped to admire the dramatic sunset, reflected in the glistening blanket at our feet. Other skiers passed us, heading toward the warmth of the inn. As we were about to follow, Bill Koch glided up to our group. In his relaxed, disarming way, he chatted with our students about skiing. Then, with a grin he said, "I guess it wouldn't look too good if I let my group get away from me." With a couple of powerful skating strides, he was gliding effortlessly across the golden snow.

"There," I remarked as our students watched him into the distance, "that's all there is to it." I turned to see Susan's smiling face in the sunset, her eyes brimming with tears.

Sometimes, cross-country skiing is an intensely beautiful sport.

Celebrate Winter

Remembering Ned Gillette

Like everyone else who knew him, I was shocked in August of 1998 to learn that Ned Gillette had been shot and killed while trekking with his wife in Pakistan. Years earlier, when Ned began his career of expeditions and adventures, many of us feared he might fall into a bottomless crevasse or be swept away by an avalanche. But as the number of his amazing outdoor achievements continued to grow, largely due to his meticulous planning, we began to think of him as invincible. It no longer surprised me to open an issue of *National Geographic* and learn that he had been the first to ski the tallest mountain in China, or had rowed from Chile to Antarctica, or had walked the ancient Silk Route from the Orient to the Mediterranean.

Originally, Ned and I were adversaries. He was Dartmouth's top cross-country skier while I raced for Middlebury at a time when those two schools dominated eastern collegiate skiing. As I recall, he missed the racing season his junior year, due to appendicitis. That allowed Middlebury to defeat our Big Green rivals a couple of times in his absence. But he roared back his senior year, reestablishing his dominance in cross-country, and capping off his college career with a decisive victory at the NCAA Championships.

That spring I was surprised and honored to be included in Bill Kendall's wedding party. Bill was one of Ned's teammates at Dartmouth. Prior to the rehearsal dinner, we escaped to an abandoned quarry where a dozen of the top collegiate skiers in the country looked fearfully over a sheer stone cliff to the water far below. As the rest of us struggled to summon our courage, Ned grinned, let out a whoop, and jumped. It was also Gillette, at the gala reception a day later, who made certain that the members of the wedding party ended up in the swimming pool, tuxedos and all.

During the summer of 1967, Ned and I trained together for several weeks in hopes of making the Grenoble Winter Olympics team. We worked hard all day at a construction site, then Ned would set the pace for our evening workout. I learned a great deal from Ned about commitment, focus, and discipline.

173

After several weeks, he announced we were ready for a break, and invited me to his family's place on Cape Cod. I assumed we'd be relaxing for a few days on the beach, but I should have known Ned better by that time.

The Gillettes owned an elegant wooden sailboat that they raced with the help of family members and carefully selected friends. Since I lacked sailing experience, Ned's first objective was to conduct a little evaluation. It was a wild, stormy day, ideal for Ned's purposes. We released the beautiful boat from her mooring, wrestled a sail up the mast, and pounded out of the harbor through the whitecaps.

Once he had room to maneuver, Ned ordered me to the pulpit, the forwardmost point of the bow railing, which actually extended beyond the deck. Over the roar of wind and waves, he instructed me to face the stern, brace my feet on the gunwales, and lean out into the pulpit. I was suspended over the raging dark water and swirling foam. Back in the cockpit, drenched with rain and seawater, Ned resembled Captain Ahab. But his face radiated a joyful excitement, and his teeth flashed through a broad grin.

"Whatever happens, don't let go," he roared above the storm. Then he turned the boat into the onrushing waves. Immediately, the bow plunged deeply, and I was completely submerged. I came up gasping through the foam and gulped a breath before another huge swell engulfed me. I can remember wondering what might happen if I did let go, but I was reassured by Ned's unrestrained laughter each time I spotted him through the seawater and foam.

Part of our training for the Olympic team back in '67 was a timed run up Mount Moosilauke. It is a tradition the Dartmouth skiers have kept alive for more than thirty years. As I joined them in the autumn of '98, a young undergraduate was handing out strips of green cloth, which the athletes knotted around their tanned biceps.

"What's this for?" I asked.

"In honor of a former Dartmouth skier who was killed in Pakistan," the young student responded.

I smiled as I tied on the armband. Ned Gillette was a dozen years out of Dartmouth before these kids were born, but already he was one of their heroes. Ned would have gotten a great laugh out of that.

Skiing Across Finland

Four decades of Nordic ski racing had taken me to most of the greatest ski centers in the world, but somehow I had missed Finland. This was a significant gap in my skiing experience, since the Finns are as fanatic about cross-country skiing as they are about their sauna baths. A friend from Maine solved this embarrassing shortcoming when he cajoled me into joining a dozen of his other gullible friends for the *Rajalta Rajalle Hiihto*, or the Border to Border Ski Tour. The borders in question were the Russian and Swedish, separated by 444 kilometers (that's about 275 miles) of frozen Finnish countryside.

The overnight flight from J.F.K. to Helsinki was smooth and uneventful, thanks to a sleeping pill and my chain-saw ear protectors. After a day of sightseeing in the Finnish capital, we boarded a domestic airliner for the one-hour flight to Kuusamo, within sight of the Russian frontier and just south of the Arctic Circle.

We were bused from the snowbound airport to a nearby sports center and assigned four into a room, though each room was clearly designed to accommodate two. But the evening meal was hearty and delicious: stew and salad, with a variety of whole grain breads and delicious cheeses. After dinner we attended an organizational meeting with our fellow ski adventurers: 37 Finns, 20 Swiss, 13 Germans, 2 Danes, 7 Swedes, 5 Canadians, and 19 Americans. I was reassured to see that many, perhaps 50 percent, were veterans of several previous Border to Border Ski Tours. At least there appeared to be survivors.

The following morning at 6 o'clock, the adventure began in earnest. We packed quickly and loaded our gear on the buses that would meet us every evening at our overnight destination. Then, it was back to the dining hall to shovel in as much oatmeal, bread, cheese and coffee as our stomachs and ski suits would allow, as well as filling our packs with sandwiches, fruit and chocolate to fuel us until evening. By 8 o'clock we were on the buses and headed for the Russian border near Saunavaara.

We disembarked at a small military outpost that overlooked a broad swath, cut through the dense evergreen forest and dotted with tall

175

watchtowers rising above the trees. Before we newcomers could fully appreciate our surroundings, the veterans were double poling down the road and out of sight. This event may have been promoted as a tour, but I have certainly seen plenty of races that were far less competitive at the start.

Soon, however, I could appreciate the veteran's eagerness to get on the trail. Although we would occasionally enjoy the beautifully groomed double tracks of commercial cross-country ski centers, the vast majority of our route was single file, in tracks set through deep powder by a snow machine. Once underway, it was difficult to pass, except at the refreshment stations provided by the organizers every 15 kilometers or so. Even though we weren't technically racing, we became so protective of our positions on the course that we rarely stopped for more than a gulp of warm lingonberry juice and a fist full of pickles, apparently a Finnish tradition for endurance events.

As if a week of skiing 55 to 75 kilometers a day wasn't enough of a challenge, on our second night, the flu bug hit. Dozens of skiers, including several of the Americans, were stricken with vomiting and diarrhea. Many had to forgo the skiing and ride the support bus to the next destination. Say what you will about the latest diet fad, but nothing takes the pounds off like skiing across Finland with the stomach flu.

Working so hard every day, you'd think we would have slept like babies. Not exactly. The accommodations were rustic and often cramped. One night, toward the end of the trip, eight guys were squeezed into a small bunk room, crisscrossed by a makeshift clothesline, festooned with our crusty ski clothes. Can you imagine the noise generated by eight, exhausted, snoring skiers? Any guesses how many times eight middle-aged men get up during the night to use the bathroom? You get the picture.

So, arriving on the Swedish border in Tornio, after seven grueling days of cross-country skiing, remains one of the most satisfying images in my memory. The endless snow-covered lakes and bogs, the countless cups of lingonberry juice, the heaping bowls of boiled potatoes: would I ever do it again? Absolutely.

A Reluctant Olympic Volunteer, Converted

I've had issues with Salt Lake City for decades. During the years I coached the Dartmouth Ski Team, the NCAA Championships were dominated by the University of Utah, but they achieved that success by recruiting most of their athletes from Scandinavia.

Then there were the back room deals the Salt Lake Olympic Bid Committee made years ago to push Anchorage, Alaska, out of the running. Anchorage was America's choice for the '92 and '94 Games, but their candidacy was blind-sided by Salt Lake, which then became the successful bidder for 2002.

Just before Salt Lake was awarded the Winter Games, a friend and I contacted Tom Welch and Dave Johnson about designing the Olympic Nordic ski courses. They planned to establish the Olympic trails on a golf course between Salt Lake and Park City, then restore it for golf immediately following the Games. When we rated the golf course as an unsuitable location for the Olympic Nordic venue, for a wide variety of reasons, Welch and Johnson made it clear we wouldn't be working for the organizing committee.

This turned out to be a blessing in disguise, since Johnson and Welch are the same two who were under indictment for orchestrating the Olympic bribery scandal that rocked the Salt Lake Organizing Committee to its core.

So, when my friend Max Cobb, chief of competition for the Olympic biathlon events, asked me to serve as chief of course, I was reluctant. But Max reminded me: this was not just Salt Lake's Olympics, it was America's Games. We were expected to host the best possible competitions for the athletes of the world, while at the same time returning to our guests the hospitality that American athletes had enjoyed in Europe for decades.

The national biathlon championships in February of 2000 served as our first test event. It poured rain for five days straight at Soldier Hollow just prior to the competitions. But when the weather turned cold, snow guns ran around the clock, and dump trucks hauled snow from a nearby mountain pass. I was thoroughly impressed by the effort.

In March 2001, Soldier Hollow was the site of a biathlon World Cup event, an opportunity for the top international competitors to experience the Olympic venue, as well as a dress rehearsal for the hundreds of volunteers who would conduct the Olympic events. The World Cup was a tremendous success.

A year later, the world had changed. Chain-link fences, metal detectors, surveillance helicopters, and security officers were everywhere. But the Games went on. From the perspective of the athletes, the thousands of spectators lining the courses, and the millions of TV viewers around the world, the Olympic skiing events at Soldier Hollow really were "the best ever."

For hundreds of volunteers, it truly was "a once in a lifetime experience." Only the ongoing scourge of illegal doping marred the nearly perfect events. I'm not embarrassed to admit that I was a reluctant Olympic volunteer at first, but in retrospect, I'm grateful to have been a part of the 2002 Salt Lake City Winter Games.

The Real Olympic Scandal

I had to smile when the Salt Lake Olympic bribery scandal made international headlines. Tom Welch and Dave Johnson of the Salt Lake bid committee might have been overzealous in their efforts to win the favor of increasingly greedy members of the International Olympic Committee, but wining and dining VIPs in an effort to earn their votes is certainly nothing new.

And to be candid, the location of the Games doesn't significantly change the conduct of the events, at least from the perspective of the athletes. Regardless of where the Games are held, the Olympic venues are well prepared, the volunteers are well trained, and local fans are gracious and hospitable.

No, I smiled at the uproar over the Salt Lake bribery fiasco because the media got everyone riled up over the wrong Olympic scandal. The truly insidious skeleton in the Olympic Committee's closet is illegal performance enhancement, or doping. Unlike bribing officials to influence where the Games are held, illegal doping undoubtably affects the results of competitive events. Simply stated, cheaters are often awarded medals, as well as the media attention that accompanies that success, while dedicated, ethical athletes, who play by the rules, are regarded as losers. Sadly, doping has become so common that the IOC and the governing bodies of the various Olympic sports are afraid to open Pandora's box, knowing that the extent of the problem will shock even the crustiest cynic.

As the eyes of the world focused on Sidney for the first Olympiad of the twenty-first century, both *Time* magazine and *Newsweek* devoted significant space to the issue of doping. In well-researched and articulate articles, both national publications outlined the most common types of illegal performance enhancement.

Anabolic steroids are usually synthetic derivatives of testosterone, taken by athletes to increase muscle mass and strength. In sports where power and strength are essential, steroids can be administered during the off season, to maximize training and to speed recovery. The drugs are discontinued prior to the competitive season, and thus undetectable during major events, like the Olympics.

Human growth hormone occurs naturally in the body and helps to maintain normal growth from infancy to adulthood. Synthetic hGH was developed for people whose normal growth has been interrupted, but used by athletes, hGH and its sister drug, insulin growth factor 1, increase muscle size and strength dramatically. Since hGH and IGF-1 occur naturally in the body, the Olympic Committee has yet to develop a foolproof test for their misuse as performance enhancers.

To a significant degree, success in endurance events depends upon the athlete's ability to supply oxygen to the muscles. Almost thirty years ago, a Swedish physiologist withdrew a unit of blood from an endurance athlete, separated the red blood cells from the plasma, and put them on ice. After a month of continued training, the athlete's red blood count had returned to normal levels. Then the physiologist reinfused the previously removed red blood cells.

In laboratory tests, the athlete's endurance improved up to 25 percent after receiving the supplement of his own red blood cells. Blood doping is nearly impossible to detect since it involves no foreign or synthetic substances.

Erythropoietin, or EPO, is a synthetic drug that stimulates the body's production of red blood cells. Developed initially for patients with anemia or kidney disease, a marathon runner taking EPO can improve by as much as four minutes. Although the Olympic Committee has celebrated its test for EPO, experts agree, unethical athletes can easily avoid detection by weaning themselves off the drug a week or so before the Games.

Like most Americans, I spent hours in front of the television during the Sidney Olympics. But far too often, I'm afraid, I wondered if the smiling medal winners earned their victories ethically or if the drive for success became so overpowering they succumbed to the temptation of illegal doping.

A Tribute to a Couple of Flatlanders

You don't have to spend too much time in northern New England before overhearing the locals make disparaging remarks about "Flatlanders." This derogatory term is usually directed toward visitors or seasonal residents from more urban areas in Massachusetts, Connecticut or New York. Often the Flatlanders are well-heeled, but woefully ignorant concerning rural living. Among the pursuits held sacred by northern New Englanders, high on the list would certainly be logging and Nordic skiing. Any Flatlander foolish enough to challenge the northerners at their own game is destined to fail. But I know of two exceptions.

Bob Haydock is a computer programmer from Concord, Massachusetts. He remembers family vacations to Woodstock, Vermont, when he was a boy. As a kid, he had to get an early start at the Suicide Six Alpine ski area, because by noon the tow rope would be too heavy for him to hold off the ground. When his dad bought an old hilltop farmhouse in Barnard, it became a Haydock family tradition to ski the six miles down the valley to Suicide Six. One day, just to see if he could do it, Bob skied back to the house from the ski area, and thus began a lifetime devotion to cross-country skiing.

Since his conversion to Nordic, Bob Haydock has volunteered in a variety of capacities. He has used his computer skills to establish a ranking system for Nordic racers. He was one of the original board members of the New England Nordic Ski Association, and until recently he chaired its Masters Committee. Through the years, he has coached young Nordic skiers of all ages, donating his time in summer at dryland training camps and in winter at competitions. Somehow, he has also managed to remain one of the top racers in his age group, routinely whipping determined rivals from the frozen north, often in spite of snowless winters in eastern Massachusetts.

But perhaps Haydock's greatest contribution to the sport is the annual Bogburn. Following his dad's example, in 1964 Bob bought a 1790's hilltop farm in Pomfret. Even before replacing the rotting sills or shoring up the tired woodshed, the Haydock family began cutting a ski trail. Nearly twenty years ago, they invited some friends over for a race and the event has steadily grown since then. In recent seasons, as many as two hundred Nordic skiers, from grade-school beginners to college hotshots and even a handful of Olympic Team veterans, have followed the hand-painted signs to a windswept hilltop in Pomfret.

The other Flatlander who deserves recognition prefers to remain anonymous. This fellow grew up in an urban part of southern New Hampshire that is today jokingly referred to as Northern Massachusetts. Some of the most vivid memories of his childhood are of family camping trips in the White Mountains. Although his career in the computer industry took him to Chicago, he never lost his love for the outdoors. When he'd had enough of the rat race, he didn't buy a yacht and retire to the Caribbean; he returned to New Hampshire and invested in 25,000 acres of forested land. He hired a respected consulting forester and directed him to develop a management plan that looked a thousand years into the future. But in addition to quality timber production, the plan is also devoted to improving wildlife habitat, as well as providing opportunities for human recreation.

Snowmobiles have used the logging roads on this fellow's woodland for decades, but recently he decided to create some trails exclusively for skiing. Soon, he was hooked on skiing, and has since developed more than 25 kilometers of beautiful trails that he grooms almost daily, as a service to the local community. The only fee he charges for this amazing recreational facility is "a smile."

No doubt, folks who have lived in the Twin States for generations have good reason to be wary of people "from away," who roar into town, throw around a lot of money, and want to change everything. But I know a couple of Flatlanders who have made tremendous contributions to their adopted, rural communities, and who demonstrate the highest standards of stewardship on their land. My hat's off to them both.

Good Times at the Winter Special Olympics

For those of us who love outdoor sports, this winter was beginning to look like a big disappointment. Barren ground kept Nordic skiing facilities closed through New Year's, and warm temperatures restricted snowmaking efforts at the Alpine resorts. By mid-January we had only a couple of inches of snow over a bulletproof crust. Some of us were feeling pretty depressed. But I found a cure.

The temperature at the base of the Dartmouth Skiway on the blustery morning of January 20 was 14 degrees Fahrenheit, and the wind chill at the top of the mountain was ten below.

But you couldn't tell that from the cheerful faces of more than 160 competitors and nearly 200 volunteers gathered for the Fifth Annual Special Olympics Upper Valley Winter Games, a festival of Alpine skiing, snowboarding, cross-country skiing and snowshoe racing for individuals with developmental challenges. In spite of the biting wind, the Skiway was packed with eager athletes, volunteers and spectators, all energized by the pure joy of sport. It would be impossible to determine which group benefitted the most from the experience: the volunteers, the participants or the spectators.

Games Director Peter Bleyler, a Dartmouth alum whose daughter, Tracy, would represent the USA at the World Games in China the following summer, leveraged his Big Green connections to recruit two hundred volunteers who did everything from setting slalom poles and timing snowshoe sprints to making seven hundred sandwiches for lunch.

Then there was the unabashed excitement of the athletes. When complemented on her impressive finish in the 50-yard snowshoe event, nine-year-old Darian Deluca from Peterborough, New Hampshire, modestly beamed, "It's my first day on snowshoes!" Then she rushed off to congratulate her best friend, Samantha Gray. Brandon Towne, another athlete from Peterborough, dominated his heats in both the 50- and the 100-meter snowshoe sprints. After his events, Brandon confirmed the obvious: "I'm fast," he said.

The final group consisted of spectators. Many were friends and relatives of the athletes, whose response, when asked about the Special Olympics was simply, "It's wonderful, fantastic!" Other spectators included local groups and teams who attended every year to cheer. The young women of Hanover and Lebanon's ice hockey teams made the finish line of the snowshoe race sound like a Bruins game in the old Boston Garden. As awards were being distributed, cocoa was being sipped, and mittens were disappearing forever under an incredible pile of winter clothes, the beautiful new McLane Family Lodge was bursting at its seams.

It was easy to imagine the founders of Dartmouth skiing—Fred Harris, Walter Prager, Otto Schneibs and Al Merrill—all smiling with satisfaction. In fact, standing virtually unnoticed in the crush was Tiger Shaw, America's top Alpine skier at the Calgary Olympics and a multiple national champion. It's really all about the joy of participation. The Special Olympics pledge states it perfectly: "Let me win. But if I cannot win, let me be brave in the attempt."

It was good to be reminded that you don't always need perfect conditions to have a great time.

The Lure of the Craftsbury Marathon

I've been cross-country skiing for forty-five years, and I've been trying to understand both the attractions of and the obstacles to the sport for much of that time. On the positive side, the aerobic health benefits of Nordic skiing have been well documented. In no other sport is the participant's cardiovascular system stimulated in a more positive way, in a given duration of time. Because it's such good exercise, cross-country skiers are often surprised by how warm they are, even on frigid, winter days. As the idyllic cover photos on skiing and outdoor magazines confirm, there is no better way to explore the silent beauty of a brilliant winter day than gliding over the powder on a pair of skinny skis.

In spite of the undisputed joys of recreational skiing, cross-country racing offers a unique set of challenges. For openers, Nordic racing is tough. With many sports, a would-be participant can simply enter an event, suit up and have fun. I don't play golf, but some of the best fun I've had in sports took place in a best ball, shotgun start, charity golf tournament in which I astounded my foursome by sinking a couple of putts. If you aren't physically fit, you don't jump in a cross-country ski race and have lots of fun.

A second challenge confronting skiers is the need to master a relatively sophisticated technique, in fact two distinct techniques — the old classic kicking and gliding as well as the newer skating, or freestyle. A Nordic racer might be very well conditioned, but unless he or she can efficiently transfer that power to the snow with good technique, the athlete's strength and endurance is squandered. Cross-country skiing is far more unforgiving in this regard than running, for example.

As if conditioning and technique were not enough of a challenge, consider waxing. In classic competitions, the objective is to wax the ski bases both for maximum glide (that is, minimum resistance to the snow), while at the same time providing adequate kick or grip to efficiently stride up the hills. In most snow conditions, it's remarkable how well modern ski waxes accomplish these seemingly contradictory tasks, but things get

185

tricky in changing weather conditions or the significant variations in elevation within a cross-country course. Waxing for Nordic races is an almost comical combination of science, art, experience and superstition: for some participants an exhilarating puzzle, for others a dreaded nightmare.

The Craftsbury Marathon, in 2008 celebrating a quarter century of showcasing the winter charm of Vermont's Northeast Kingdom, always seems to provide an ample supply of both the attraction to and the challenges facing Nordic skiing. Thanks to adequate snow cover in early December, Nordic enthusiasts throughout New England were able to get a jump on their training for Craftsbury's demanding 50-kilometer or 25-kilometer course. The field is limited to one thousand entrants, and with the advent of online registration, the available slots go fast.

As the Groundhog Day race date approached, Mother Nature interceded with characteristic unpredictability. The abundant early season snow was nearly erased by a strong January thaw. Then high winds covered the trails with branches, boughs and debris. The forty-eight hours before the race included sleet, hail, freezing rain, and a soaking rain, followed by some powder snow. Thanks to an impressive effort by John Brodhead, his support crew, and dozens of volunteers, the course was ready for a start that had been delayed two hours, giving competitors additional time to negotiate the icy roads to the event.

The scene at the Highland Lodge moments before the start was a classic, waxing panic: racers anxiously testing their skis, coaches frantically torching on (or in some cases, scraping off) klister, while athletes with no-wax race skis smugly stretched and loosened up. Most experienced competitors acknowledged that there wasn't any combination that would work well for the entire course. The trick was to find something that worked reasonably well for most of the race.

For the next two-and-a-half (for the top competitors) or five hours (for the admirably determined ones), participants made the best of it, many stopping to rewax, refuel with energy drink or simply socialize with the enthusiastic volunteers manning the aid stations.

The 2008 Craftsbury Marathon was not one of those beautiful, cold powder kind of days, but most of the participants would be back the next February. They'd return to the Northeast Kingdom for the scenic beauty, for the opportunity to test themselves against a challenging course, and for the chance to reconnect with longtime friends and Nordic enthusiasts.

Celebrate Winter

Warren Chivers

Maybe I was developing a "glass half empty" perspective, but the sports headlines were pretty discouraging. After a phenomenal comeback in one of the toughest mountain stages, Lance Armstrong's heir apparent in the Tour de France, an American named Floyd Landis, went on to win the event only to be disqualified a few days later when a doping test revealed elevated levels of testosterone, and *synthetic* testosterone at that.

Meanwhile, in track and field, multiple Olympic medalist Marion Jones was making a comeback after being hounded out of competition by allegations that she had been supplied illegal performance enhancements by BALCO founder, Victor Conte. Ironically, the same day Jones won the 100-meter sprint at the U.S. Track and Field Championships, traces of EPO were revealed in her drug test. She faces a two-year ban from competition.

On the men's side, Justin Gatlin, who shares the world record in the 100 meter and was an outspoken critic of illegal doping, received an eight-year ban for failing a drug test back in April 2006. It was Gatlin's second offense. He was also stripped of his world record. And over on the soccer pitch, with billions around the globe watching on TV, French star Zinedine Zidane was ejected from the World Cup final for head-butting an Italian opponent. Zidane was a pro, some have said the best player of his generation, so his lapse of judgment and breach of sportsmanship in what should have been his finest hour, was inexcusable. I can't believe that in his long career of combat on the soccer pitch, it was the first time he had heard insulting comments about his mother or his sister from an unethical opponent.

Ironically, what turned my attitude around was a memorial service. Warren Chivers, former Dartmouth skier, 1936 Winter Olympian, as well as longtime coach and outdoor educator at Vermont Academy in Saxtons River, died August 18, 2006, at the age of 91. A week later, friends, relatives, former students, and teaching colleagues gathered under large tents erected on VA's athletic field to celebrate the life of a legitimate American skiing legend.

In 2005, Warren's skiing accomplishments were enumerated when he was inducted into the Vermont Ski Museum's Hall of Fame. He was a four-event competitor at Dartmouth (slalom, downhill, jumping and cross-country) and captain of the ski team. He competed in the Nordic combined events at the 1936 Winter Olympics in Garmisch-Partenkirchen, Germany, while serving as an alternate on the Alpine squad as well. He was the national cross-country champion in 1937. In 1940, Chivers again earned a spot on the Olympic team, but World War II forced the cancellation of those Games. He was inducted into the U.S. National Ski Hall of Fame in 1971.

Following a five-year hitch as a naval officer, Chivers married and accepted a teaching and coaching position at Vermont Academy, where he would raise his family and exert a positive influence on hundreds of young students. Under his low-key but capable leadership, Vermont Academy set the standard for competitive skiing during the 1950s and '60s.

Chivers' protegees included Mike Gallagher, who led U.S. cross-country skiers to three Winter Olympics and coached at a fourth. Marty Hall was a champion four-event skier under Chivers, then went on to coach successful U.S. and Canadian Nordic squads internationally for two decades.

C. B. Vaughn, for a time holder of the world speed record on skis and also founder of CB Sports, a highly regarded manufacturer of ski clothing, credits Chivers with teaching him the skills needed to succeed.

There were damp eyes and speakers pausing to gather their composure as they shared memories of Warren Chivers, but there was also plenty of laughter and genuine admiration for a champion who dedicated his life to passing along his love for the sport of skiing. It was a timely reminder that although the cheaters and the showboats might attract the media attention, there are still plenty of dedicated, capable coaches and educators out there, making important contributions every day that enhance our enjoyment of sport and enrich our lives.

Thanks, Warren. Keep 'em pointed downhill.

Minnie Dole, the National Ski Patrol and the Tenth Mountain Division

In the winter of 1936, Charles Minot Dole, a frequent visitor to Vermont, was skiing Mount Mansfield with his wife and another couple when an unfortunate event led to a series of great ideas. In those days, before chairlifts and grooming machines, skiing was a rough-and-tumble sport, demanding hours of arduous hiking in exchange for a few moments of exhilarating descent.

When Minnie Dole (as he was known to his friends) fell and broke an ankle, the wives were sent for help. They returned hours later, empty handed except for a piece of tin that served as a splint. Nine weeks later, Dole's skiing buddy, Frank Edson, was not so lucky. Hurt in a more serious fall, Edson died, and Minnie Dole resolved to do something about ski safety.

In 1938, he organized a ski patrol for the national downhill races held at Stowe; then, later that year, with ninety-four volunteers, he established the National Ski Patrol. Today, the National Ski Patrol is comprised of nearly thirty thousand men and women serving on six hundred ski patrols throughout America. It has pioneered innovative approaches to outdoor emergency care, evaluated ski equipment, developed avalanche rescue techniques, and promoted safety in both Alpine and Nordic skiing, and more recently, snowboarding.

But the ski patrol was only one of Minnie Dole's good ideas. In the winter of 1939, the Soviet Union invaded Finland. Small units of Finnish soldiers on skis were able to annihilate two Russian tank divisions, humiliating the invaders. Minnie Dole saw the Finnish Winter War as justification for establishing a mountain warfare unit in the U.S. Army.

The War Department was not easy to convince, but after months of persistence, Dole was able to present his plan to General George C. Marshall, the army chief of staff, who recognized its merit. The day after the attack on Pearl Harbor, the army activated its first mountain unit, the Eighty-seventh Mountain Infantry, at Fort Lewis, Washington.

The outfit quickly became known as Minnie's Ski Troops, since Dole and his National Ski Patrol assumed responsibility for recruiting qualified young men for the unit. Skiers and outdoorsmen from across the country traveled to Mount Ranier where the Eighty-seventh was training. In July of 1943, the Eighty-seventh was relocated to Camp Hale, Colorado, and expanded into the Tenth Mountain Division.

Finally, after years of training, in January 1945, the Tenth was deployed to the mountains of Italy, where it saw fierce combat and took heavy causalities as it drove the Germans north to the Po Valley.

When those ski troops returned to civilian life after the war, they developed ski resorts, established ski schools, imported equipment from Europe, and manufactured ski clothing here in the U.S.

It could be said that thanks to Minnie Dole's broken ankle on Mount Mansfield, the National Ski Patrol was created, the Tenth Mountain Division was established, and Vermont's ski industry today ranks third in the nation, pumping $1.4 billion annually into the state's economy.

The Dog Dilemma

I love dogs! As a kid, I had a beagle named Buddy who spent endless hours exploring the nearby woods and fields with me. During my high school years, our family was challenged by the antics of Rusty and Dusty, sibling golden retrievers who proudly displayed trophy woodchuck carcasses on the back step and frequently returned from adventures with their shaggy coats encrusted with burdocks and cow manure.

Within a week of my release from active duty in the army, I was riding my bike home from classes at the University in Anchorage when I passed the city's animal shelter. Out of curiosity, I pulled in for a look. It was pitiful seeing the rows of cages, filled with dogs of all sizes, yipping and jumping for attention. The lone exception was an enclosure labeled "Pure Lab, female," which contained a small mound of black fur in the far corner of the cage.

"Is this one really a pure lab?" I asked the attendant.

"Yup, she's the last one of a litter left by a military family that had to ship out on short notice."

"What's wrong with her?" She was the only dog in the shelter not barking or jumping enthusiastically.

"She's exhausted. The staff has been playing with her all morning, out back on the lawn."

"Could I talk it over with my wife and pick up the dog tomorrow?"

"Nope, she's scheduled to be put down this afternoon. If you want this dog, you've got to take her with you right now."

I knew that one of the unfortunate realities for many animal shelters was euthanizing unwanted stray dogs and cats, but confronting that reality firsthand really had a profound impact. I filled out the paperwork, paid the fees, put the bundle of fur in my backpack and peddled home. It turned out to be one of the best spontaneous decisions I have ever made. Rode became a constant running and hiking companion, an alert watch dog and a valued member of the family. When she died, there was a considerable void in our household, which eventually was filled by Klister, another black lab.

Klister picked up where Rode left off, eagerly hiking for hours with the family in the White Mountains or launching herself, full speed, off the dock into the pond. Klister was with us for more than a decade, and when she died, I was afraid I had used up my quota of really great dogs. Then my wife, Kay, spotted an ad for a "short-haired retriever," a breed I'd never heard of. We went to see the puppy at our local veterinarian, a sensitive but no-nonsense woman who had cared for both Rode and Klister. The short-haired retriever turned out to be a yellow lab, and again, we took her on the spot. Rosie has lived up to the high standards set by her two predecessors, and then some. Not only does Rosie love running and hiking with the family and chasing squirrels on her own, but Rosie is especially enthusiastic about cross-country skiing.

Ah ha, finally, the dilemma! Few activities give me more satisfaction than kicking and striding along freshly groomed, classic tracks in cold powder snow. I've been spoiled, thanks to my participation (in various capacities) in dozens of major competitive events, at which teams of grooming experts spent every night creating absolutely flawless, classic ski tracks.

During the past few winters, I have joined a couple of friends in an attempt to provide better skiing in our community by grooming three local trails. While it is satisfying to set beautiful classic tracks in fresh snow, it is equally frustrating to see skiers with their dogs obliterate those tracks before they've had a chance to firm up.

So as a devoted dog lover and a Nordic skier, I offer the following suggestions to promote harmony on the trails. If you ski with your dog, seek out a trail that welcomes pets. Some Nordic centers have a designated pet loop; others permit dogs on certain days of the week. Carry a supply of plastic bags and clean up after your dog. Use small treats to train your dog to behave when you encounter other dogs or skiers. Finally, use discretion when taking your dog on a groomed trail. If the snow is fresh and soft, paw prints can ruin the tracks, while firm snow conditions can be nearly impervious to dog prints. Celebrate winter!

Skiing Loses a Couple of Stalwarts

Most skiers in the Northeast had sore faces from smiling at the remarkably abundant snowfalls of the winter of 2008. With all the legitimate evidence of global warming, and the apparent weather trends of the decade, few of us believed we'd actually experience a "good, old-fashioned, New England winter" ever again. I know the deep snow puts a strain on wildlife, depletes the plowing budgets of rural communities and even threatens charming, historical buildings. But what a joy the snow was to winter sports enthusiasts!

For skiers though, the four-month celebration of Mother Nature's bounty was tempered by the loss of two beloved champions, Dr. David Bradley and Paul Robbins.

Dave Bradley died on January seventh near his home in Norway, Maine. He was 92. Talk about living life to the fullest and being an eyewitness to history, Dave set the bar pretty high. He was an English major and captain of the ski team at Dartmouth College. In 1938 he graduated summa cum laude, the same year he was named national champion in the Nordic combined (cross-country and jumping). Along with his younger brother Steve and seven other Dartmouth teammates, Dave was named to the 1940 Winter Olympics team, but robbed of the opportunity to compete by World War II.

Following Dartmouth, Dave studied English and history at Cambridge University before traveling to Finland where he reported on the Russo-Finnish Winter War for several midwestern newspapers. Returning to the States, he attended Harvard Medical School, earning his M.D. in 1944. He joined the army and was assigned as a medical officer to the atomic tests being conducted on the remote, South Pacific Bikini Atoll. Based upon his journal, in 1948 he published *No Place to Hide*, the first authoritative, widely read, eyewitness account of the potential catastrophe of the atomic age.

In 1960 Dr. Bradley returned to Finland where he taught English for two years at the University of Helsinki. He also served as team manager of the U.S. Nordic skiers at the Squaw Valley Winter Olympics. For decades, he was a strong advocate for ski jumping, serving each winter as a jumping judge at competitions throughout the Northeast, and designing or reconfiguring more than sixty jumping hills. Trudging up the stairs of the landing hill, if a glance at the judge's stand revealed Dave Bradley's weathered face, usually with a pipe clenched in his teeth, you knew, regardless of how far you flew down the hill, you'd better throw in a solid Telemark landing, or you were going to get docked plenty of style points.

Paul Robbins was not himself a champion skier but for more than thirty years was America's most outspoken champion for skiing. Paul was a graduate of Holy Cross and served as a press officer for the U.S. Army in Korea. He was introduced to skiing in the late 1970s when Wisconsin entrepreneur Tony Wise recruited Paul to promote the World Cup cross-country races being held at Telemark Lodge in Cable. Through hard work, an amazing ability to remember facts, and his infectious sense of humor, Paul soon became the spokesperson for Nordic skiing in North America. His articles appeared in a wide variety of publications including magazines, newspapers and official press guides.

His comprehensive knowledge of Nordic skiing and sincere affection for the athletes led to a twenty-year affiliation as the primary writer for the U.S. Ski Team. Paul was a predictable fixture at every Winter Olympic Games since Lake Placid in 1980, not only writing daily updates for newspapers back home, but also serving as an expert analyst for the television networks covering the Nordic events.

I served as the team leader for the U.S. biathletes at three Winter Olympics, responsible among other things for managing the athletes' interactions with the media. For many sportswriters, the Olympics are a junket, an opportunity to escape the routine of football, basketball and baseball. As a result, few were knowledgeable about Nordic skiing, and their questions to the athletes were painfully naive. At the obligatory press briefings, I would frantically scan the assembled reporters for Paul's signature plaid tam o' shanter, knowing I could count on him for an insightful question.

At the biathlon team's press conference at the Lillehammer Games, the very first question to our panel of athletes was "What do you think of this whole Tanya and Nancy controversy?" Without missing a beat, Curtis Schreiner, one of our veteran competitors, responded, "Who are Tanya and Nancy?" Most of the reporters in the room stared at Curtis in disbelief, since the media had been obsessed with the figure skaters for weeks, but Paul Robbins roared with laughter because he alone knew that Curtis was yanking everyone's chain.

Paul passed away on February twenty-third, at his desk, writing about skiing. He will be sorely missed by Nordic skiers across North America.

Celebrate Winter

Drama and Sport

Although in high school and college I occasionally enjoyed student theatrical productions, I never had much in common with my classmates who were into drama. They appeared to take themselves too seriously, they stayed up very late arguing obscure interpretations of some playwright's intentions, and most of them smoked. Of course, the theatrical crowd didn't have much use for us jocks either. We were frequently stereotyped as too dumb to discuss anything except sports, more concerned with getting ten hours of sleep then cramming for an exam, and far too focused on health to smoke or even drink coffee.

I remained relatively unshakable in my view of the theater crowd until I met my wife Kay, who is every bit as passionate about the theater as I am about sports. Kay has been performing on stage since high school and her credits include an impressive list of community theater productions, small parts in a couple of movies, a few TV commercials, and in the summer of 2007, rave reviews as a contestant in the Prairie Home Companion, Norway Fjords Cruise talent show. For many years Kay taught drama and directed middle school musicals.

What has emerged in our marriage is a greater appreciation of the similarities between a devotion to the stage and to the ski trail. For starters, both athletes and thespians work very hard at their craft. As a former Olympic biathlete, I thought I knew about long hours of training prior to an important race, but my focus on skiing and shooting is nothing special compared to the time and energy Kay invests in memorizing every word of an eighty-page script.

Kay loosens up before a performance with stretching, verbal agility drills, and finding a quiet place to focus, very similar to how many athletes prepare for a competition.

The cast of a play, along with the backstage and technical crew, all function as a highly skilled team. And like an athletic team, the cast of a play has problems if one of the actors tries to hog the spotlight in the same way a team suffers if a player won't pass the ball to his or her teammates.

Conversely, Kay has expressed great admiration for actors who have the stage presence to smoothly adjust and cover for a colleague who may have dropped a line, not unlike an athlete making the best of a bad pass.

Kay and I have had interesting discussions about directors and coaches. The similarities between these two roles are striking, but perhaps not surprising, since the goal of both is to guide and encourage talented people to perform at their optimum level, often under considerable stress. We shared memories of wonderful coaches and directors whose insight and selfless dedication inspired their athletes and actors to strive for the Olympics or for Broadway. We also recalled less gifted individuals in both domains, tyrants who had lost perspective, living out their own unfulfilled dreams through the young people under their care.

Of course, some sports, like figure skating or synchronized swimming, are by nature more dramatic. A friend of mine who works for the U.S. Olympic Committee once confided that he had misgivings about any sport in which the athletes were as worried about their makeup as their results. But I guess to be fair, I'd have to admit that the black stuff on Tom Brady's cheeks probably qualifies as makeup, of a sort.

On the other hand, there are probably a lot of dedicated athletes who could not endure the physical challenges of performing with a top-flight ballet company. Although I've never been a big ballet fan, there is no question that those jumps, spins and lifts require tremendous strength, poise and athletic ability. There was a story a while ago that one of the top NFL teams hired a ballet instructor to help their receivers and running backs become more agile in evading defensive players. The team results improved, and the ballet classes were no longer a source of jokes and ridicule.

Kay and I have achieved an admirable level of mutual respect. She has eagerly embraced Nordic skiing, participating in the Canadian Ski Marathon the past few years. For my part, I attend, and usually enjoy, a lot more theatrical productions than I ever did before.

Sports Fans: The Good, the Bad and the Ugly

Although it may already be relegated to ancient history, like many sports enthusiasts, I became engrossed in the 2011 Stanley Cup finals between the Boston Bruins and the Vancouver Canucks. Televised ice hockey typically isn't much of a draw for me, but two loosely related issues pulled me in. Early in the series it was mentioned that Tim Thomas, the star goalkeeper for the Bruins, was a graduate of UVM, so I was eager to see how a player with strong ties to Vermont fared on the international stage. Needless to say, Thomas did very well, leading Boston to victory and earning recognition as the most valuable player of the championship series.

I also had a soft spot in my heart for Vancouver, since that city had done such a remarkable job hosting the 2010 Winter Olympic Games. My wife, Kay, and I spent a wonderful week at those Olympics, which included the very exciting early round men's ice hockey matchup between Team USA and the host Canadians. A small group of us in red, white, and blue were engulfed by a sea of red and white maple leaves, many of whom were amply fueled by Molson's and LaBatt's. At one point during the game, when the young guys behind us returned from the concession stand with yet more refreshment, one of our group bravely turned and requested that the beer didn't end up all over us. The Canadians laughed heartily.

As you may recall, that first cross-border matchup of the 2010 Olympics ended in a victory for the U.S., thanks in large part to the heroics of the U.S. goalie. As we filed from our seats, I risked a subdued comment to the stunned Canadian fans a row behind us, "Sorry about the final score, but it was a hell of a hockey game."

"Aw, don't worry about it mate," came the immediate response, "we'll get you in the gold medal round." Which of course they did, in dramatic fashion.

It was especially because of this memory that I was so disappointed to learn about the violence and mayhem that followed the final Stanley Cup game in Vancouver. For several hours, the streets were filled with raging people who clashed with police, looted stores and started fires. The

201

frustration and disappointment of having the Stanley Cup snatched from their grasp so close to victory may have been the catalyst for the violence that followed, but a frightening example of mob mentality quickly took over.

I have experienced that type of outrageous behavior in other sporting events. At the 1974 World Biathlon Championships in Minsk, then part of the Soviet Union, the hosting Russian team had done poorly in the opening events. Their chance for redemption, in front of an estimated 120,000 fanatic local fans, was to defeat the arch rival Finns in the relay. The first three skiers from each team battled it out on the shooting range and the ski tracks, keeping the outcome in question until the final leg. The Soviet hero, Alexander Tikhonov, matched strides and shots with Finland's anchor, Heikki Ikola, until the final stage of shooting, when Tikhonov returned to the skiing loop first. Those were the days of sticky klister wax for icy or warming snow conditions. The course was lined with Soviet spectators. As soon as their hero passed they threw pine and spruce needles onto the tracks to sabotage Ikola's skis. After the race, Heikki confided to me, "Today, I would have feared for my life if I had won."

In contrast, I have another vivid memory, this one from the 1994 Winter Olympics in Lillehammer. The hosting Norwegians consider skiing as much a part of their heritage as the Vikings, and they had been preparing their athletes to succeed at Lillehammer for a decade. But as the Games unfolded, some of the Norwegian spectators and officials feared that they had overdone it. I remember being asked by concerned Norwegians if other countries might think that the host team was hogging the medals.

The Olympic men's cross-country relay had been a recurring battle between the Italians and the Norwegians, often resulting in a photo finish after 40 kilometers of racing. In Lillehammer, more than one hundred thousand passionate Norwegian fans screamed the two anchormen toward the line, then fell totally silent, uncertain which athlete had finished first. When the Italians were declared the winners, the Norwegian crowd remained stunned for a few seconds, then they roared their approval of one of the most exciting races they would ever see.

The Basics of Nordic Ski Trail Design

According to a number of recent studies, well-designed, carefully constructed recreational trails have become one of the leading amenities Americans seek when purchasing a new home. And while there have been significant changes in trails intended for Nordic skiing since the skating revolution of the 1980s, ski trails still have broad appeal for outdoor enthusiasts of all types, including runners, hikers, snowshoers and mountain bikers.

Following a twelve-year career as a Nordic competitor, including two Winter Olympic Games and several Biathlon World Championships, then nearly twenty years as a Nordic ski coach including over a decade as head coach of men's skiing at Dartmouth College, I discovered a small but exciting business opportunity designing recreational trails. I have designed more than two hundred trails for clients ranging from retired couples who simply want to get out into their woodlot, to organizing committees hosting major international competitions. We have had projects throughout the northern United Sates as well as in Scotland, South Korea and China. While the majority of our work focuses on Nordic skiing, we also design trails for hiking, cross-country running, mountain biking, snowshoeing and equestrian events.

Step one in the configuration of a new trail network is to determine what the client wants balanced with what the available property and terrain can accommodate. A municipality might envision an FIS homologated (approved) competition venue that could draw major national or even international events to their community, while a retired couple may simply look forward to outings in their woodlot with the grandchildren.

Once the objectives of the trail are clear, it is important to identify the boundaries of the available property. Often, adjacent landowners are also enthusiastic about trails and are willing to be part of the project. Next, an inspection of the property will reveal significant natural attractions and perhaps a few challenges. There may be impressive old trees, rock outcroppings or potential vistas that the trail should access. Conversely, there may be drainages, wetlands or roads that the trail should avoid.

A stacked loop or ladder configuration gives folks a chance to adjust their outing to their level of fitness or the time they have available by the use of cut-offs that lead back to the starting point. In a best-case scenario, the loop or loops closest to the start/finish should be the most forgiving in terms of length and terrain, while the outlying loops can be longer, with more challenging climbs and faster descents. We advocate skiing and mountain biking the trails in one direction. Climbs should be manageable, with traverses and changes of direction to keep participants from seeing the full extent of the climb — this keeps their spirits up! Descents should be exhilarating and fun — in short, worth the effort of the climb. Technical, turning descents provide a welcome challenge for advanced skiers while at the same time forcing novices into a snowplow position, which helps them control their speed before they get out of control and fall.

A frequent dilemma is how much of any existing road, logging skid trail or clearing under power lines to incorporate into a new trail network. Historically, many Nordic trails in this country followed the "path of least resistance" rather than cutting new routes through the woods. The result was often long, boring, straight sections of trail with seemingly endless climbs, followed by "white knuckle" descents that robbed the participant of a satisfying feeling of rhythm or flow.

Trail width is often a topic of discussion. While snowshoers, trail runners and mountain bikers often prefer single track, contemporary Nordic skiing requires much wider trails for three reasons. First, to accommodate both classic tracks and a skating lane the trail surface should be at least 14 feet wide. Second, trails of this width are most efficiently built by excavators, and a 14-foot trail opening gives the typical machine room to operate without scarring the bordering trees. Finally, in this era of unpredictable natural snowfall, a 14-foot trail width insures that the forest canopy above the trail is opened so that the snow that falls actually reaches the ground.

Like many examples of good design, excellent ski trail configuration can be subtle. As you enjoy the sport this winter, try to recognize if a climb seems manageable and leads to a rewarding overlook. Is the following descent so much fun that you are tempted to try the loop again? If so you are probably skiing a well-designed course.

Celebrate Winter

The Search for Early Snow

A characteristic shared by most Nordic skiers is the anticipation of getting on snow. For dedicated competitors this becomes an obsession. Swimmers, runners, and tennis players can enjoy their sports year-round, but Nordic skiers in the Northeast are typically limited to four or five months of reliable snow cover. Mother Nature can be fickle, some years rewarding skiers with cold temperatures and skiable snow soon after Thanksgiving, while other winters we are still looking at depressingly bare ground well into January.

It's ancient history now, but the Nordic events of the 1980 Winter Olympics in Lake Placid were very nearly cancelled due to a complete absence of natural snow throughout the Northeast. It was only due to the courageous and monumental effort of covering more than 15 kilometers of trail with man-made snow (which had never before been attempted) that the Nordic skiing events of that Olympics were conducted at Mount Van Hoevenberg on schedule.

What heightens the skier's anxiety is the historical inaccuracy of the long-range weather forecast. The prediction might be for a "wetter and colder winter than normal," but that doesn't necessarily translate into more snow. New England sits at the junction of two major weather patterns. Most of our weather blows in from the west. We can assume with some confidence that a winter storm battering Minnesota, Michigan and then the Finger Lakes of New York is headed for Vermont and New Hampshire. But occasionally, low-pressure systems follow the East Coast up from the Carolinas and Virginia, loaded with moisture from the Gulf Stream. If these systems collide with cold air from Canada before they reach New England, we get the legendary Nor'easters that can dump feet rather than inches of snow.

The problem is that those storms from the Midwest frequently blow themselves out in the Adirondacks or drift north into Quebec, and the coastal storms often drift out to sea before reaching the Northeast, or worse, never encounter the cold air from Canada, covering New England with heavy rain instead of snow. The result is that devoted Nordic skiers can become "twitchy" about the weather, especially early in the season.

For Olympic hopefuls and national team aspirants, the solution is to travel to reliable snow, which usually means somewhere in the Rocky Mountains, the Pacific Northwest or even Alaska. West Yellowstone, Montana, has been a mecca for Nordic skiers during Thanksgiving week for the past couple of decades, while racers in Fairbanks and Anchorage, Alaska, typically are on snow sometime in October.

Closer to home, Mount St. Anne, less than an hour northeast of Quebec City, has provided college ski teams reliable snow in early December for a generation. A couple of hours east of St. Anne, Aroostook County, Maine, has developed a couple of world-class Nordic facilities in Fort Kent and Presque Isle, which frequently provide skiing soon after Thanksgiving.

For those who can't spare a few days and the seven-hour drive north to get on snow, there are a couple of local options. Nordic enthusiasts in Stowe, Vermont, anticipate the closing of the Smuggler's Notch road. Since it is a smooth, paved surface, it requires only a few inches of dense, heavy snow to make the road skiable. A comparable paved route is the Bear Notch Road linking Bartlett, New Hampshire, to the Kancamagus Highway. A third option is the U.S. Forest Service road over the Green Mountains from Plymouth to Shrewsbury, Vermont. Since all three of these roads are closed to vehicles in winter and share a relatively high elevation, they are a good bet for early snow.

Even closer to home are the options of mowed pastures and golf courses. Since both of these options provide very smooth surfaces, a minimal snow cover can produce satisfactory skiing, if only for a few days. Early in the season, it's not unusual to find a strip of snow blown by the wind along the edge of a field or in the shadow of a stone wall. If it turns out to be one of those winters when we have cold temperatures, but no snow, it's possible to ski on little more than a heavy frost on a frozen pond.

In fact, in the late 1960s when I was a student at Middlebury College, one of my teammates discovered that Lake Plead, a small pond at the Middlebury Snow Bowl, was frozen with a couple of inches of powder. We skied there on Halloween, and never missed a day on snow thereafter. Those were the days…

Vancouver Olympics Wrap-up

When my wife Kay and I were offered the opportunity to attend the Vancouver Winter Olympics, we were thrilled. Having served as the U.S. biathlon team leader twenty-two years earlier in Calgary, I knew the Canadians would host a spectacular Games. After a roller coaster week of euphoric victories and heart-wrenching disappointments, Kay and I headed home, emotionally spent but deeply grateful for the inspiring experience. Encompassing all the impressive individual and team efforts were three themes that seemed to characterize these Games.

First was the apparent shift from the traditionally powerful Winter Olympic nations. Switzerland, France, Austria, Germany and Italy did not dominate the Alpine skiing events as in the past. In fact, the U.S. emerged as the strongest Alpine team thanks to the success of Vonn, Mancuso, Miller and Weibrecht, who won a total of eight medals.

On the Nordic side, the Soviet Union typically took home the lion's share of the hardware, with some escaping to Scandinavia. In biathlon, the unification of East and West Germany created a twenty-year dynasty. Nordic combined glory was shared by Central European and Scandinavian athletes. Johnny Spillane of Steamboat Springs, Colorado, signaled an end to that tradition with his silver medal in the normal hill competition, which inspired additional podium performances from the U.S. team, including a gold for Bill Demong of Vermontville, New York. In biathlon and cross-country, Olympic medals went to athletes from Slovakia, France, Austria, Croatia, Estonia, Switzerland, Poland, Kazakhstan, Belarus and the Czech Republic in addition to the traditional powers.

A second observation was the phenomenal skill of the participating athletes. Not so long ago, a world-class biathlete was doing well to hit five targets in under a minute and cover the ski course at a rate of three minutes per kilometer. The biathletes in Vancouver routinely hit five targets in less than twenty-five seconds, while the pace in the men's 50-kilometer cross-country event was under two-and-a-half minutes per

209

kilometer in wet, slow conditions. And how about the spins, twists and flips of the freestyle skiers and snowboarders?

Our final impression of the Vancouver Winter Games was a reaffirmation of Calgary's legacy, that our neighbors to the north simply know how to organize and host a tremendous Winter Olympics. It helps, of course, to have a site among the most spectacular in the world. The jagged peaks, the massive Douglas firs and the magnificent ocean vistas quickly established our most frequent comment: "Wow!" Equally as impressive as the scenery was the efficiency and friendliness of the countless volunteers. Even a row of burly hockey fans, sitting behind us in the preliminary men's U.S./Canada game, wearing the ubiquitous maple leaf jerseys and fueled by a seemingly endless supply of Molsen, were courteous and friendly, even in defeat. Congratulations to Team USA for dramatically improved Winter Olympic results, and congratulations to Canada, for once again showing the world how the Games should be hosted.

Thoughts of Norway

Although I sometimes feel numb to the seemingly constant flow of tragic news — tornados ravaging the American South, a tsunami devastating scores of communities in Japan, and famine threatening millions in Africa — the deranged Norwegian gunman whose day-long rampage in July of 2011 killed nearly one hundred of his countrymen hit me especially hard. I have many fond memories of several visits to the birthplace of Nordic skiing, and the actions of thirty-two-year-old Anders Behring Breivik seem inconceivable in the nation that gave the world the Lillehammer Winter Olympics and the Nobel Prizes.

Although grandparents on my mother's side came to this country from Sweden, and there has always been a spirited rivalry between the Swedes and their neighbors to the west, I have long had a fascination with Norway. As a high school then collegiate cross-country skier, I was familiar with the top Russians, Finns, Swedes and Germans, but it was the Norwegians, like Odd Martinsen, anchor of their formidable relay team in the late 1960s, whom I tried to emulate.

In the summer of 1966, like many American college students, I stuffed some clothes and a couple of maps in a backpack, bought a low-budget plane ticket and set out to hitchhike around Europe. It didn't take me long to get to Norway. On the outskirts of Oslo, a family leaving on holiday gave me a lift. The mom cheerfully squeezed in the back seat with her kids, allowing me the opportunity to chat with her husband as he drove north. They gave me good advice about where to stay, historic points of interest and natural wonders.

A group of local Norwegians at the youth hostel in Lillehammer invited several of us foreign travelers to join them on a hike to a nearby waterfall and swimming hole. After an hour or so of brisk walking into the nearby hills we reached a mountain stream, tumbling over a rock outcrop to a pool below, that was worthy of a cover photo on a national tourist brochure. Laughing and shouting encouragement, our Norwegian guides stripped off their clothes and plunged into the icy water. Some of the European hostel guests quickly followed the Norwegians' example. Ever since, I've regretted that bashfulness or my New England, Puritan upbringing caused me to hesitate then hike back to the hostel without swimming. Those Norwegian kids seemed to display a wholesome innocence that is rare in our country.

Through several years of international competition on the U.S. biathlon team I became friends with a few world-class Norwegian skiers. Kjell Hovda, like many of his teammates, was in the military. Following the 1976 Olympics in Innsbruck, he invited me to stay for a few days at his home in Honnefoss, a couple of train stops north of Oslo. Hovda was a far better biathlete than I, so I was eager to pick up some training pointers. One morning he suggested a "tour" from his hometown, down through the famous Nordmarka Park to Oslo. As we began our workout, I was baffled by his modest pace. Almost 100 kilometers later, I was barely hanging on while Kjell effortlessly maintained the same pace he had established hours earlier.

The 1994 Winter Olympics in Lillehammer showcased the Norwegians at their best. In near perfect winter conditions the home team excelled, winning medals in nearly every discipline, while hundreds of thousands of rosy-cheeked, flag-waving, winter sports fanatics lined the courses cheering for all the competitors, regardless of nationality. Their speed-skating icon, Johann Olav Koss, donated $30,000 following his first gold medal performance to Olympic Aid, a charity he helped establish to benefit youth in war-torn nations of Africa and Eastern Europe. Thanks to Koss' efforts, before the Lillehammer Olympic torch was extinguished more than $1 million had been raised for Olympic Aid.

A couple of summers ago, my wife, Kay, and I had the good fortune to join the Prairie Home Companion Norwegian fjord cruise. Daily excursions to the towns and scenic wonders of Norway's convoluted west coast, supplemented by evening entertainment on the ship by Garrison Keillor and the performers from his weekly NPR radio show, created a once-in-a-lifetime experience. On an afternoon hike in the warm sunshine above Kristiansand, Kay and I rested on a warm rock. Soon, we were both asleep, sensing, perhaps, the security of the Norwegian culture, even in a popular public park.

It is especially sobering to recognize that senseless violence can strike anywhere, even in a place as idyllic as Norway.

Memorable Biathlon Events Bookend the Season

I can't help one look back at the remarkable 2010–2011 ski season. The snow may have been late in arriving here in New England, but when it came, we were buried. Locations to the south and over near the Atlantic coast, which typically have decent skiing only a couple of weeks each winter, were grooming trails for months, in old fashioned, deep powder conditions.

Partly due to coincidence, my winter was "bookended" by two biathlon events, which make for some interesting comparisons. The first was the Biathlon World Cup in early February at the Nordic Heritage Center in Presque Isle, Maine. Since the January storms went well south of Aroostook County, the dedicated volunteers who hosted the event worked hard to cover the race course with machine-made snow. By the time the European teams arrived, Mother Nature made a modest contribution as well, so at least it looked like winter across the potato fields and into the forests of northern Maine.

Following the example of World Cup sites in Germany and Scandinavia, Presque Isle and Fort Kent (a week later) scheduled community festivals around the biathlon races. There were the colorful opening ceremonies, dogsled demonstrations, sleigh rides, art exhibits, quilt shows, a hypnotist, a wide assortment of musical groups, and of course, fireworks. At the competition venue it was possible to watch the athletes practicing their marksmanship on the shooting range, while coaches and waxing technicians repeatedly rode skis through speed traps to determine the fastest wax.

Race days were a kaleidoscope of activity, color and sound. Upbeat music filled the stadium when the announcers weren't alerting the spectators to developments during the race. Busloads of schoolchildren in colorful hats cheered for foreign athletes whose home countries they had studied. A jumbo television screen showed fans at the shooting range what was going on out on the ski course. The competitions were a blur of some of the world's fastest Nordic skiers as well as some very exciting shootouts on the range, where several athletes arrived together and the most poised,

213

accurate shooter left with a clean target while the others, perhaps rattled by the pressure, missed targets and circled the penalty loop.

The spectators were hoping to see an American on the podium, which wasn't to be at this World Cup, but most of us came away encouraged by the grit of the U.S. athletes we watched compete. In this intensely competitive sport where a millimeter on a target can mean the difference between a medal and the third page of the results, the U.S. team was steadily gaining ground on the Europeans.

Late in March, I had the opportunity to travel to southern California to help at another biathlon race. Four years prior, Dr. Mike Karch, an orthopedic surgeon who has served as the physician for the U.S. Nordic combined team, organized an invitational biathlon event in his community of Mammoth Lakes. Mammoth Mountain, founded decades ago by Alpine skiing pioneer Dave McCoy, is also noted for its mind-boggling snowpack. Just over the mountains, to the east of Yosemite, it is not unusual for Mammoth to have 20 feet of snow on the ground in March! This year was especially bountiful, even by local standards, and several of the cabins at the Tamarack Lodge were accessed only by tunnels that had been carved deep into the drifts.

In the four years that Mike hosted his biathlon event, it had grown to involve more than two hundred competitors. There was a novice, youth category, where the youngsters shoot laser rifles on an abbreviated range (to promote initial success in hitting the targets). This year, several members of the Wounded Warriors of the Eastern Sierra (a program devoted to helping disabled combat veterans rediscover the joy of sport) participated to the thunderous encouragement of the assembled spectators and other racers.

As frequently is the case in the Sierras, a blizzard blew in on Saturday, forcing a revision from biathlon races to cross-country skiing events. Although the howling wind and thick snow made seeing the targets impossible, dozens of competitors skied through the storm and will no doubt be talking about their experience for years. Sunday broke clear and brilliant. As if skiing fast and hitting the targets were not enough of a challenge, the course was located at 9,000 feet above sea level. Dozens of biathletes, from first-time shooters to former Olympians, racing in waves of twenty, experienced firsthand just how difficult it is to hit those targets, especially shooting with a high pulse in a gusty wind.

Vancouver Olympics team members Wynn Roberts and Lanny Barnes took top honors in the men's and women's elite events, edging out fellow national team members, Raleigh Goessling and Susan Dunklee. Additional favorites with the boisterous crowd of spectators included 1980 Olympic biathlon alumnus and longtime coach of the Farwest junior team, Glenn Jobe, frequent summer biathlon champion, Marc Sheppard, and 1972 Olympic contender, Pat Armstrong. The enthusiastic fans also cheered loudly for the several medical professionals who were no doubt cajoled into participating by the charismatic Dr. Karch. One woman, obviously new to the sport, smiled philosophically as none of her targets fell, "Why does that damn penalty loop have to be right in front of the crowd? It's so embarrassing!" I tried to reassure her that she would have plenty of company on the loop due to the altitude and the gusty winds.

It was a terrific event, especially considering the remarkable diversity of experience and ability represented by the participants. Thanks in large part to an energetic, local "Pied Piper," winter biathlon has developed an enthusiastic following in the mountains of California. It's safe to say that coast to coast, biathlon has arrived in the U.S.

Celebrate Winter

What Winter?

The winter of 2011–2012 began with real promise a couple of days before Halloween, by dumping a foot of heavy, wet snow throughout much of New England. Many skiing enthusiasts realized that it would probably melt (it was only October, after all) but a genuine snowstorm that early in the season had to be a good omen. I remember a winter during my college years, maybe 1967, when one of my teammates discovered a frozen pond near the spine of the Green Mountains with a dusting of snow that provided excellent early season training. We skied there on Halloween and for several days thereafter, until snow covered the cross-country trails lower down the mountains.

So skiing in October wasn't unprecedented. But Mother Nature was cruel to Nordic skiers in the winter of 2011–2012. The October snowfall quickly melted, thanks to record-setting warm temperatures in November. In fact, five of the last six days of the month were above 60 degrees in Boston! The trend continued through December, making it the sixth warmest on record with no measurable snowfall.

Well, we've had late winters before, certainly the pattern would change in January. Nope! Across the nation, 2,892 record-high temperatures were recorded in the first month of 2012, according to the *Wilcox Journal*. Boston received half an inch of snow on January tenth, and another 2.9 inches on the twenty-first, putting it on track to set an all-time record for minimal snowfall. February was virtually dry as well, until the evening of the twenty-ninth, when nine-tenths of an inch was recorded, which ultimately pushed the season total to 9.1 inches, a mere tenth of an inch over the previous record set in the winter of 1936–1937.

I'm a fan of Bill McKibben, both because of his persistent efforts to draw public attention to the growing threat of climate change, and because he is also an avid Nordic enthusiast. McKibben's book *Eaarth* definitely got my attention. It seemed even more prescient after tropical storm Irene's devastating impact on the Northeast and the uncharacteristically warm temperatures and minimal snowfall of 2011–2012. Those politicians who continue to doubt the reality of global warming simply have to get out of their offices more often. For Nordic ski enthusiasts, I'm afraid the future looks bleak.

But it may not be time to trade your skinny skis for a bowling ball. As many of us have noted, there are pockets in the Northeast that, for reasons of geography or weather patterns, seem to receive and retain more snow than the regional average. In addition, there are several Nordic facilities that have invested in snow-making technology, which they use to great effect when the temperatures permit, insuring reliable cross-country skiing, in spite of Mother Nature's stinginess.

Ironically, 2011–2012 was a terrific winter for skiing in Europe: cold temperatures and plenty of snow. In fact, the countries of Eastern Europe suffered the most severe winter in memory. Hundreds died in the bitter cold and tens of thousands were snowbound for days.

These conditions boded well for U.S. Nordic skiers competing in European World Cup events throughout the season. Of special note was Alaskan Kikkan Randall, who won the season-long World Cup sprint title. She was America's first Nordic skiing World Cup Champion since Vermont's Bill Koch won the 1982 overall World Cup title. In addition to her sprint championship, Kikkan finished fifth in the women's overall World Cup standings, the best international ranking ever for an American female cross-country skier. Joining Kikkan, five other U.S. women and five U.S. men scored World Cup points, moving the U.S. to eighth in the Nations Cup standings, up from fifteenth just two years prior.

On the biathlon side, the results were almost as impressive. In her rookie season on the World Cup circuit, Susan Dunklee of Barton, Vermont, had a fifth place finish at the World Championships in Rupholding, Germany, best ever for an American woman. Russell Currier of Stockholm, Maine, enjoyed a breakthrough season, featuring an exciting sixth place World Cup result in Nove Mesto, Czech Republic. In fact, during the World Cup season, there were fourteen top-ten World

Cup and World Championship finishes, by five different American biathletes, including seven top-six finishes. Two American men finished the World Cup season in the top twenty overall: UVM grad Lowell Bailey in fourteenth, and Tim Burke of Paul Smiths, New York, in twentieth.

With results like those, we couldn't give up on winter. Instead, we made reservations for Sochi!

Celebrate Winter

"Two Roads Diverge..."

I recently became aware of an interesting divergence of philosophies regarding competition trails for cross-country running and Nordic skiing. Some time ago, I was invited to consult on the creation of a national caliber cross-country running venue in Louisville, Kentucky. A new race course was to be part of an ambitious, nationally prominent urban park, and created with an eye toward hosting major national and even international cross-country running events. The University of Louisville, famous for its impressive sports programs, including successful football and NCAA championship basketball teams, is also noted for its excellent cross-country runners. Their coach boasted years of experience at the elite level of the sport.

Therefore, it came as a surprise to me when he suggested the course should be "flat and fast." Typically, cross-country courses reflect the local terrain and topography of the specific location. In other words, elite runners competing in Kansas or Indiana would expect a relatively flat race course while athletes running a course in West Virginia or Vermont would expect hillier terrain. It is the endless variety of the various courses that is one of the attractive aspects of the sport.

The Louisville coach suggested I visit the LaVern Gibson Championship Cross-Country Course in Terra Haute, Indiana, which has hosted many competitions, including several NCAA championship events. I was both impressed and a bit puzzled by what I found. The Gibson venue is a jackpot for spectators, who can see virtually the entire race course from near the start/finish area. The site consists of 280 acres of reclaimed coal mine and land fill, purposely devoid of trees or anything that would obstruct the view of the spectators. The course is virtually straight and relatively level for nearly the entire first kilometer, giving the athletes plenty of distance to sort themselves out from the starting line to the first turn.

But what really surprised me about the championship course in Terra Haute is that it is relatively flat. Although the site might be described as very gently rolling, there is nothing on the course that a runner from Vermont would describe as a hill. Later, the Louisville coach confirmed that the current trend in elite, cross-country running is for fast times, which translates into flat courses.

An interesting side note to this refinement of the sport is the desire for a uniform, preferably grass, running surface. Although cross-country running evolved a century ago in Great Britain on rough, hilly trails, complete with stream crossings and vaulting of stone walls, more recently in the U.S. the only available open area in urban communities was the golf course. As a result, cross-country in the States often meant running down manicured fairways, which has become a desired attribute of championship trails designed for the sport. A cynical traditionalist might complain that cross-country running has become more like a track meet on grass.

In contrast, cross-country ski racing has headed in the opposite direction. Anyone who watched the Nordic skiing events of the 2014 Sochi Olympic Games or the 2018 PyeongChang Olympic Games had to be aware of the increased technical and physical challenge of the courses. It was not long ago that a typical cross-country ski course consisted of one-third climb, one-third descent and one-third relatively flat skiing. Except for a few hundred meters at the start/finish area, the level skiing has largely disappeared from the equation. Modern ski trails focus on physically punishing climbs, often followed by fast, technical descents. Thanks in part to warm temperatures, inconsistent snow conditions, and especially challenging courses, Olympic Nordic enthusiasts see a relatively high number of falls, some of them resulting in injuries.

I believe this tendency to increase the difficulty of the world-caliber Nordic ski courses is driven by two factors. First, the capability of the elite athlete has steadily and dramatically improved. Barely a generation ago the men's 50-kilometer event was a monumental survival test that could take four hours. Now, thanks to advancements in ski construction, waxing technology and snow grooming, in addition to the capabilities of the athletes, the Olympic 50 kilometer seems more like a sprint, usually with more than a dozen racers in contention for a medal. The second factor, for better or worse, is television. All Olympic sports are competing with each other for air time, and it's clear that the viewing audience enjoys the rough and tumble of snowboard cross and the (probably made for TV) slope style.

As a devoted Nordic skier and since 1978 a Vermonter, I find it discouraging that some influential collegiate cross-country running coaches are taking some of the challenge, tradition and essence out of their sport by advocating manicured, flat courses.

Celebrate Winter

Discovering Yet Another Joy of Cross-Country Skiing

Cross-country skiing has been a part of my life for over half a century, and as I approached the start of my seventh decade, I had assumed that I had experienced just about all the rewards that the sport had to offer. I remember being an eager high school skier, long on enthusiasm but short on talent, thrust into a cross-country race in place of an injured teammate, and discovering to my astonishment that pushing hard had a positive impact on the result. For a kid who was pathetic in junior high basketball and baseball, who "played" four years (mostly junior varsity) high school football on the bench, and who still holds a school tennis record by losing thirty-two consecutive singles matches over four years, this revelation that success was possible in Nordic skiing, simply through hard work, was transformational for me.

By my sophomore year in college, I had earned a spot on the varsity team but was by no means exceptional. That year, the final winter carnival of the collegiate season (which was also designated as the Eastern Intercollegiate Championship) was hosted by Middlebury at their Bread Loaf campus near the spine of the Green Mountains. As I recall, it was snowing hard and we were scrambling to find a wax that worked well in the accumulating powder. It was all classic technique back then; skating wouldn't emerge for another decade. I believe we started at minute intervals, so in the falling snow, we were completely alone within seconds of leaving the starting gate.

I remember thinking a worthy goal for the race would be to hold off the good skiers who started behind me for as long as I could, then, as each tracked me, to hang on to them for as long as possible. But a couple of kilometers into the race, before I heard any panting from behind, I spotted a ghostly shape through the falling snow on the trail ahead. I soon recognized the skier as Brian Beattie, one of Dartmouth's top racers and a member of the U.S. Nordic combined team. At first, I was terrified that if I had caught Beattie so soon, I must have started much too fast, and would certainly burn out long before the end of the race. But I didn't feel winded, so I respectfully tracked Brian and got an encouraging remark in return. From then on, it was full speed ahead. I never felt tired. I just seemed to fly through the snowstorm. No one was more surprised than I to learn when the results were posted that I had finished first, ahead of several more experienced skiers. In the decades since, whenever I hear of any athlete (a golfer, basketball player, major league pitcher, even a NASCAR driver) being "in the zone" and appearing to win effortlessly, I know exactly what they are describing.

Although racing and training for competition constitutes the majority of my time on skis, there have been plenty of memorable recreational outings. Fifteen years ago, several Nordic skiing friends encouraged me to join them in an event called the "Ski Across Finland." For a week in March, two hundred cross-country skiers, representing more than a dozen nations, skied from the Russian border near Kuusamo, 444 kilometers west to Tornio, on the Swedish frontier. We ate reindeer stew washed down with blueberry juice. In the evenings, we restored our aching muscles in stifling hot saunas, followed by rolling in the deep snow. This was a week of kicking, gliding and double-poling through a part of the world where skiing is not just a sport, but has been a central part of the culture for centuries.

There have been many other adventures and escapades on skis through the years, but few have brought the joy of one of my recent outings. My granddaughter, Hazel, who is not yet two and a half, loves the outdoors, winter, and skiing. Her parents have bundled her up, tucked her into a pulk (a small fiberglass Scandinavian sled designed to be pulled behind a cross-country skier) and taken her out on the trails. But Hazel prefers to have the cold air on her rosy cheeks and to see where she's going, so I offered to carry her in a backpack. There is an entirely new level of enjoyment in having the small voice of your granddaughter squealing in your ear, "Faster, Papa, faster! More downhills, more downhills…!"

Original Publication

Some of the pieces included in this collection had a previous life either as a radio commentary or as a column in a newspaper or magazine.

The following originally aired on Vermont Public Radio's Commentary series.

Lessons from Lillehammer, May 3, 1994

Showing Off, May 31, 1994

The Joys of Roller Skiing, August 2, 1994

Victory in the Sauna, August 16, 1994

The Frogman and the Physicist, December 13, 1994

The Dunkin' Donut Challenge, December 27, 1994

Back to Zakopane, January 10, 1995

Report from the Skunkworks, February 7, 1995

The Art and Magic of Waxing Cross-Country Skis, February 28, 1995

The Legacy of Annie Oakley, June 13, 1995

Of Scholar Athletes and Commencement at Dartmouth, June 27, 1995

Patty Sheehan the Ski Jumper, July 23, 1995

Endurance Feeding, January 23, 1996

Dipping the Flag, February 20, 1996

Sometimes the Excitement Is Traveling to or from the Race, March 19, 1996

Passing the Torch, April 25, 1996

Gloria, May 21, 1996

To Survive, or to Celebrate Winter, That Is the Question, February 4, 1997

A Day on the Catamount Trail, February 5, 1997

A Beautiful Day at the L.L.Bean Ski Festival, December 9, 1997

Team Leader, December 30, 1997

Nagano on TV, January 27, 1998

Ecstasy and Agony in Bozeman, September 8, 1998

Remembering Ned Gillette, January 12, 1999

Nordic Skiing Returns to Aroostook County, 2000, March 3, 2000

The Real Olympic Scandal, September 14, 2000

Roller Skiing in Vermont, September 27, 2000

John Caldwell's Wild West Tour, November 30, 2000

Finnish Skiers Open Pandora's Box, April 17, 2001

A Reluctant Olympic Volunteer, Converted, April 3, 2002
Minnie, Dole, The National Ski Patrol and the Tenth Mountain Division, December 2, 2002
The Drama of Choosing an Olympic Team, January 11, 2006
Good Times at the Winter Special Olympics, February 18, 2007
Skiing Loses a Couple of Stalwarts, March 21, 2008
The World Returns to Aroostook County, 2010, March 3, 2010
Vancouver Olympics Wrap-up, March 5, 2010
Some Friendly Coaching for Russia's President Medvedev, March 26, 2010

The following were originally published in *Vermont Sports Today*.
Report from the Skunkworks, December 1992
The Dunkin' Donut Challenge, December 1995/December 2001
Showing Off, January 1996
Passing the Torch in Canmore, February 1996
The Joys of Roller Skiing, December 1996
Dipping the Flag, January 1997
Ecstasy and Agony in Bozeman, November 1997
To Survive, or to Celebrate Winter, That Is the Question, November 1997/October 2000
Endurance Feeding, April 1998
A Beautiful Day at the L.L.Bean Festival, December 1998
The Art and Magic of Waxing Cross-Country Skis, January 1999
A Day on the Catamount Trail, February 1999
Sometimes the Excitement Is Traveling to or from the Race, March 1999
Remembering Ned Gillette, April 1999
John Caldwell's Wild West Tour, November 1999
The Frogman and the Physicist, February 2000
Back to Zakopane, March 2000
Nordic Skiing Returns to Aroostook County, 2000, September 2000
Roller Skiing in Vermont, November 2000
Victory in the Sauna, April 2001
Finnish Skiers Open Pandora's Box, July 2001
The Real Olympic Scandal, November 2001
Skiing Across Finland, January 2002
Team Leader, February 2002
Nagano on TV, March 2002

A Reluctant Olympic Volunteer, Converted, April 2002
Minnie Dole, the National Ski Patrol and the Tenth Mountain Division, January 2003
A Tribute to a Couple of Flatlanders, February 2003
A Reunion in Alaska, August 2003
The Drama of Choosing an Olympic Team, February 2006
Memories of Beirut, September 2006
Warren Chivers, October 2006
Dartmouth Skiers Win the NCAA Championship, May 2007
Vancouver Olympic Nordic Preview, November 2007
Goal Setting for Nordic Skiers, January 2008
February Memories, February 2008
The Lure of the Craftsbury Marathon, March 2008
Drama and Sport, May 2008
Let the Women Jump, February 2009
The Dog Dilemma, April 2009
The Search for Early Snow, December 2009
A Skier's Guide to the Vancouver Olympics, February 2010
The World Returns to Aroostook County, 2010, September 2010
Memorable Biathlon Events Bookend the Season, May 2011
One of the Rewards of Coaching, June 2011
Sports Fans: The Good, the Bad and the Ugly, August 2011
Thoughts of Norway, September/October 2011
What Winter?, June 2012
U.S. Skiing Loses a Couple of Champions, January 2014
The Russian Riddle, April 2014
"Two Roads Diverge...", June 2014
Discovering Yet Another Joy of Cross-Country Skiing, February 2015

The following was originally published in *VFW Magazine*.
The Origins of Olympic Biathlon, February 2014

The following was originally published in the *Valley News*.
Back to Zakopane, January 16, 1994

The following was originally published in the *Middlebury College Magazine*.
Patty Sheehan the Ski Jumper, Winter 1996

The following was originally published in *Faster Skier*.
Reflections of an Old-Timer at the PyeongChang Winter Olympics, March 2018

The following was originally published in *Cross-Country Skier Magazine*.
The Basics of Nordic Ski Trail Design, Winter 2017

The following were originally published in *Master Skier* magazine.
The Art and Magic of Waxing Cross-Country Skis, Preseason 1995
Sometimes the Excitement Is Traveling to or from the Race, Preseason 1996/1997

Acknowledgments

This collection of stories and essays would not have been possible without help, encouragement and advice from a number of people: Betty Smith-Mastaler, who for decades was the demanding but supportive producer of the Vermont Public Radio commentary series, Kate Carter, the founder and skillful editor of Vermont Sports newspaper, as well as Angelo Lynn, the current publisher of Vermont Sports.

I am also grateful to Jason Albert, Lowell Bailey, Tim Burke, John Caldwell, Sarah Clarke, Max Cobb, Tyler Cohen, Joni Cole, Casey Dennis, Sean Doherty, Susan Dunklee, Tim Dyhouse, Peter Graves, Bob & Nancy Gregg, John Griesemer, Marty Hall, Deborah Heimann, Trina Hosmer, Matt Jennings, Jim Kenyon, Dan Kuzio, Karl Lindholm, Bernie Marvin, Kay Morton, Emily Newton, Matt Senger and Steve "Monk" Williams.

About the Author

John Morton has participated in ten Winter Olympic Games as an athlete, a coach, the biathlon team leader, chief of course or, more recently, enthusiastic U.S. biathlon team fan. He has attended scores of national championships, world championships, biathlon world cup competitions, and the World University Games.

After 11 years as head coach of Men's Skiing at Dartmouth College, he wrote *Don't Look Back*, a comprehensive guide to cross-country ski racing. In 1998, he published *A Medal of Honor*, a novel about the Winter Olympics. He has been a commentator for Vermont Public Radio, a regular columnist for *Vermont Sports* (a monthly newspaper) and his articles on the outdoors have appeared in more than two dozen publications.

Morton is also the founder of Morton Trails, and has spent the past thirty years designing nearly 250 recreational trails and competition venues across the country. He currently has projects underway throughout the northern USA and in China. More information regarding his trail design work can be found at www.mortontrails.com. He lives with his wife Kay, at the end of a dirt road in Thetford, VT, surrounded by trails.